A FELINE AFFAIR

A FELINE AFFAIR

A Guide To

Raising and Breeding Purebred Cats

by

ELAINE WENNER GILBERTSON

Foreword

by

Richard O. Wattles, D.V.M.

Illustrated
by
Dari McKee

Alpine Publications Inc.

P.O. Box 7027 · Loveland, CO 80537 · (303) 667-2017

Library of Congress Cataloging-in-Publication Data

Gilbertson, Elaine Wenner, 1916–
    A feline affair : raising and breeding purebred cats / by Elaine
Wenner Gilbertson ; foreword by Richard O. Wattles ; illustrated by
Dari McKee. — 1st ed.
        p.   cm.
    Includes bibliographical references and index.
    ISBN 0-931866-62-6
    1. Cats—Breeding. 2. Cats. I. Title.
SF447.5.G54   1993
636.8'08'2—dc20   93-24226
                                                                        CIP
Cover Design: Bob Schram/Bookends
Front Cover Photo: Robert & Eunice Pearcy
Back Cover Photo: Author and **Rajapur's Turbo**, Himalayan Flame Point male kitten,
OW: Michael Mullikisa & Chris Hoffman, PH: Ron Burgis

Explanation of abbreviations used in photo captions: CH—Champion; GC—Grand
Champion; SGC—Senior Grand Champion; MGC—Master Grand Champion; GP—
Grand Premier; PR—Premier; BR—Breeder; OW—Owner; PH—Photographer.

Printed in the United States of America
First Edition
1 2 3 4 5 6 7 8 9
ISBN: 0-931866-62-6

ACKNOWLEDGMENTS

My gratitude to:
  Leone Stein, the cat-friend who started it all
  Dari McKee, for her imaginative illustrations
  Richard O. Wattles, DVM, for his medical help
  The breeders and photographers who contributed so generously of
    their time and talent
  Grandson Nick for "computerizing" his Nanna
  Daughters Diane, Wendy, and Joy for their encouragement
  My husband for his patience and understanding
  Most of all, my mentors, the Himmies of Rajapur, who taught me so
    much about the world of cats

CONTENTS

FOREWORD

As the popularity of the cat, as a household pet, has grown enormously over the past two decades, so have the periodical literature and reference works written about the cat. Another cat book may seem to add to the redundancy, but the author has found a need and filled it. The emphasis is on the purebred cat, but the majority of information can be applied to the domestic breed. The chapters on feline reproduction and viral diseases are extremely current, reflecting new advances in veterinary medicine. Interestingly, up until the 1980s, significant parts of the feline reproductive cycle had remained a mystery to veterinarians and physiologists. Many breeders and veterinarians had often wondered why so many queens seemed never to go out of heat! Also a mystery is the development of the Feline Immunodeficiency Virus (FIV), which although distinct from the human AIDS virus, has many parallels to the human virus in its evolution.

When first asked to review the manuscript for accuracy in the medical sections of the book, I had no idea of what I would find inside. I had known Elaine Gilbertson for over 10 years, not only as a client and ardent cat enthusiast, but also as a dedicated and conscientious breeder of Himalayan cats. I was most pleasantly surprised to find that she writes with a light and humorous style that is most entertaining. The book can easily be read by a complete novice in the field of purebred cats. Her explanations of the unique feline quirks are straightforward and lucid. Even a new cat owner will sense the guiding hand of her experience in most of the common feline encounters. Experienced cat breeders will also find the book useful for both an update to their knowledge and for the enjoyment of the "cat experience," which all cat lovers enjoy sharing.

In my own practice I have clients asking me for references that would guide them through the purchasing, breeding, queening, and raising of purebred cats. Previously, I had no recommendations, but now I do. Elaine Gilbertson has combined a wealth of experience and common sense to create a written work that I can recommend to anyone who has a serious or even casual interest in learning more about the purebred cat.

Richard O. Wattles, D.V.M.

INTRODUCTION

I love cats. I've always loved cats. As a child I adopted strays, sometimes with parental permission, sometimes not. As a bride, I coaxed my husband into letting me keep a homeless kitten who promptly became "our first baby." A succession of tolerant cats were trundled about in doll carriages by a succession of three small daughters. As the years scampered by, new generations of felines invaded slumber parties to snuggle in sleeping bags with giggling teenagers. Suddenly, or so it seemed, there were grandsons shinnying up trees to rescue "Nanna's stuck cats," and granddaughters spoon-feeding kittens in dolly highchairs.

It was inevitable that my love for cats would evolve into a vocation wrapped around the breeding and showing of purebreds. It was just as inevitable that eventually I would write a book about them.

Pets have always been an integral part of the American scene. Dogs were favored until the past decade, when canine popularity slumped and the popularity of cats rose by more than 20 percent. This swing of the pet pendulum was undoubtedly caused by the realistic needs of today's frantically busy world.

Except for fish (and how can you hug a fish!) the easiest animal to care for is the cat. It adapts to limited space, making it an excellent apartment pet. Through climbing, stretching, and romping, a cat exercises itself, thus eliminating the chore of daily walks. Most felines are quiet in voice and movement, a boon to the neighbors as well as to owners arriving home from a nerve-racking day on the job.

Because of the cat's fetish for personal cleanliness, it exudes little or no body odor and requires only occasional bathing. As a kitten, it trains readily to the litter box. If the box is properly maintained, elimination habits remain faultless.

Those of us pressed for time, money, or space appreciate feline eating habits. A cat's table manners are impeccable. Seldom do they gorge or slobber—rather, they *nibble,* a practice that minimizes cleanup as well as waste. Cat food can be purchased in small cans and compact boxes that take little space in a crowded cupboard. And one can feel easy leaving one's cat alone for a day or two, knowing its contentment in dry food snacking.

These are a few of the *practical* advantages of cat-ownership. Of even more import are those feline intangibles that lift human spirits and warm human hearts.

Cat-ownership is really a misnomer—no one *owns* a cat. A cat will be your friend but not your property. That marvelous independence is what attracted so many of us in the first place. Groveling or begging is contrary to feline nature, although a cat will put on a pretense of fawning to get what it wants. Despite a surface aloofness, a cat is capable of great affection, whether for an individual or humans in general. My Snow Poppy typified the "people-puss," delightedly greeting visitors and hamming it up for cat show audiences.

A cat plays many roles. It can be a companion to the lonely, a tonic for the invalid, a stimulant to the depressed. A cat's purring is not only sweet to the ear, it lowers heart rate and blood pressure. A cat can revitalize an older person; the simple fact of being needed lends purpose to getting up in the morning. When cats are brought into a prison or a home for the aged, the positive personality changes that occur verge on the miraculous.

Then there is the delight to the eye that the cat gives. With its diversity of moods, no other living creature has such beauty and grace. We see the cat as a Sphynx, sitting motionless, not a muscle, a whisker, an eyelash twitching; the cat as a tender-eyed madonna, curling her young to life-giving breasts. Or the cat as a hunter, liquid as quicksilver, flowing through mounds of autumn leaves in silent stalk of its prey.

If the *seen* of the cat fascinates, the *unseen* sweeps us from our staid urban existence into another world. The mystery of the cat conjures images of flitting shadows in dark primal jungles. In the depths of those enigmatic eyes lie glimpses of past civilizations that worshipped the cat for its inimitable beauty.

Yet a cat can be the epitome of entertainment. Clown kitten, coy maiden, or strutting tom, this mercurial animal will never be boring. One moment it may choose to caress with a rub of an arched back, the next to scorn with a flick of the tail. Ah, but the bliss of those times when it chooses to be a velvet lover, touching with a velvet paw, nuzzling with a velvet nose, murmuring endearments in a velvet voice.

Magical creature though the cat may be, it has realistic needs. With the purebred these physical and emotional needs tend to vary according to the breed. For the would-be buyer, a special section (Appendix #1) sketches the personalities, the appearance, and the idiosyncrasies of more than forty kinds of purebreds.

The selection, nurturing, and ultimate breeding of a fine cat can be a simple or an arduous procedure. This book was written as a guide. It takes the neophyte cat fancier through the capricious first months of kittenhood, past the exasperations of puberty, into the complexities of mating and pregnancy, the fulfillment of birth, and the eventual placement of the kittens. Although tailored to the specific needs of the purebred, the information and advice can be used by all cat-owners.

Not that it's necessary to follow every suggestion put forth. We live in a busy world and most of us have neither the time nor the energy to observe an exacting pet regimen. I suggest that you choose those procedures which, while providing for the basic needs of your cat, can be niched comfortably into your particular life style.

Elaine Wenner Gilbertson

To Snow Poppy
1982–1990

1
AN INTRODUCTION
TO THE PUREBRED

The Cat Show

U sually one's first purebred is a female because of the (erroneous) consensus that a female is more loving. Usually the female is a kitten because of our inherent need to nurture and to imprint with our own personality. Usually the kitten is pet quality because there's no other choice, breeders keep the best for themselves.

For a novice, selecting the right kitten from more than forty registered breeds is like picking the winning number in a lottery. Should she be a longhair or a shorthair? Large or small? Solid or patterned? Which breed is the most affectionate? Which requires the least care? Which has an affordable price tag?

A good place to learn about purebreds is at a cat show.

Purchase a magazine like *Cats* or *Cat Fancy* to find show listings. Dates, hours, and locations are specified, with most shows held on weekends. Plan to go early, to spend the entire day looking over the potpourri of cats, talking with their owners, and gathering information for later perusal.

To a newcomer a first show can be utterly bewildering. The huge hall teems like a hill of ants. Cat-carriers are stacked in the aisles. Vendors of cat products bustle around their booths. Nervous exhibitors slap last-minute touches to gaudily decorated cages or race, tray in hand, to the litter supply or feverishly groom their already impeccable cats. The jumble of sounds swells to a crescendo—cats wailing, doors slamming, voices shrilling, the loudspeaker blaring announcements. Odors of food, coffee, cigarettes, disinfectant, male spray, flea spray, coat spray, and talcum powder assail the nostrils. The first judging is announced. Spectators hasten to find seats. Exhibitors scurry by, carrying their cats as if they were precious china.

It's all part of the cat fancy, which in the form of cat clubs sponsors most major shows. It is not necessary to belong to a club to compete, but most entry rules state that a cat must be registered with the association to which the club belongs. It must also be healthy, clean, fully immunized, and (in most associations) have claws intact and trimmed. Four judgings a day are customary and a show may run one or two days.

In brief, there are three competitive divisions: *non-Championship*, *Championship*, and *Premiership*.

The non-Championship division has several categories, but entries are mainly four-to-eight-month-old kittens. These compete within their breed, sex, and color for ribbons but not for Championship titles.

In the Championship division, adults are entered by breed, sex, color, and also title. *Title* specifies whether the purebred is an *open* (or beginner), a *champion*, or a *grand champion*. An open competes against other opens until it becomes a champion; then it competes against other champions as it works toward the status of grand champion.

The Premiership is designed for altered purebreds. Judging is the same except that an alter attaining a specific number of winner's ribbons is called a *premier* or a *grand premier* instead of a champion or a grand champion.

Some shows include *Household Pets*, which compete in the non-Championship division. They must be registered as Household Pets, be altered and current on immunizations. A pedigreed cat, unregistered because it does not meet breed standards, may also compete in the HHP class.

Cats in competition are said to be *benched*, which means being assigned to a specific area in the show hall. Each entry is given a number. When the show announcer calls that number, the cat's owner takes it to the designated ring and places it in the cage bearing its number to await judging.

CH Mistymagic Prince Charming, Persian White Copper-eyed male— *BR/OW/PH: Cherie Lightner, GotTheLookCattery.*

In a one-day show four rings are customary, each hemmed by ten to twelve judging cages. A long table occupies the center of the ring. Here the judging takes place and the ring clerk records the decisions. The data are then mailed to the show-affiliated association to be filed.

The *gate* is an expression that refers to spectators, who, after paying a small admittance charge, are free to stroll the aisles of caged cats or to watch the ring-judging.

The first thing such spectators are apt to notice is the predominance of the *Persian*. These lovely, sweet-natured cats rank number one in popularity polls. Short, thick legs support a cobby body with a plump, abbreviated tail and a massive head. The small, well-rounded ears and the tiny snub nose set between large, expressive eyes make for a saucy expression. Yet this is an elegant cat with a coat so long and thick that it billows like a ball of thistledown.

A coat of such density requires daily grooming to prevent shedding and matting. The eyes may also need extra care because they tend to tear, due to the flatness of the face. If one has the time, the added care is worth it—a quiet, sensitive "lap-sitter" like the Persian is especially suitable for a single working person or an apartment dweller.

ACFA **GC-Hiwind's Luck of the Draw,** Himalayan Blue Point male—BR/OW: *Gena Windham,* PH: *Expressly Portraits.*

Another exquisite longhair is the *Himalayan.* This singular breed emerged from the mating of Persian to Siamese. One might call it "the Gemini Cat," because it unites the outstanding characteristics of its two ancestors into a charming entity. Persian mellowness and dignity mingle with Siamese sparkle and intelligence. In head and body conformation as well as in coat, the Himalayan adheres to Persian standards and is registered as such in some associations. The dazzling blue eye color reverts to the Siamese, as do the dramatic *points* (contrasting color on face, ears, feet, and tail). The delightful duality of the Himalayan cannot help but be a factor in its popularity.

A first-time show patron may mistake a *Birman* for a Himalayan. There is a resemblance, but the Birman's nose is longer and its ears larger. Even more distinctive are the white "gloves" on the feet and the "lacings" on the rear legs. Known as the Sacred Cat of Burma, the Birman's gentle and loving nature makes it an ideal family pet.

Because of its name, the Birman is sometimes confused with the *Burmese.* The differences are obvious. The Birman is a longhair with a creamy-gold coat enhanced by dark points. The coat of a Burmese

GRC Pleasantview Orinoco of Birjan
Birman, Seal Point female — OW:
Richard and Janice Mayo, BR/PH: Julie
Collin.

is short and solid in color. Both breeds boast huge round eyes, the Birman's deep blue, those of the Burmese golden.

While spectators wander the aisles of caged cats, the show rings keep occupied with the judging. Competition in one ring is entirely separate from competition in another. Because each judge rules independently, a cat winning the (CFA) blue First Place ribbon in one ring may be awarded a Third Place yellow in another. Additional ribbons hang from cages — Best of Color, Best of Breed, Best Shorthair, Best Longhair, and various others.

Confusing as the judging might be for the neophyte, even more so is putting breed names on the wide variety of cats. A simple solution is to buy a show catalog at the door. Compare catalog numbers with cage numbers to learn the breed, color, sex, and status of each entry.

For example, in Ring 2 where shorthair adults are being judged, cage #47 holds a long-bodied, orange-brown cat. In the catalog, cat #47 is designated as a Ruddy Male *Abyssinian*.

Second in popularity among shorthair breeds and third overall, Abyssinians have aptly been dubbed "Lions of Love." Long, lean muscles ripple under a crisp, ticked coat. The thin tail is tapered, and neat little tufts spring from pointed ears. Svelte and leonine, the Abyssinian resembles the Kaffir cat pictured on the walls of Egyptian tombs and indeed may have originated in or near Egypt. A runner, a leaper, and a climber, this emerald-eyed shorthair needs ample space for its high-flying feats, as well as an owner with steady nerves.

Acrobatic Abyssinian

In the same ring, #52 is listed as a Silver Tabby *American Shorthair*. Oldest of the North American cats, the American Shorthair's ancestors are reputed to have come over on the Mayflower. The thick, hard coat requires little grooming and has a wide color range. Sturdy and strong, the American Shorthair has a long life-expectancy. Although friendly and infinitely adaptable, its independent nature makes it a true Yankee cat.

Once-familiar cats are today not so familiar—like the *Siamese* presently crouched on the judging table. The apple-shaped head of the past has become a wedge. The original Siamese color was Seal Point; now the streamlined bodies are wrapped in blue, chocolate, red, or even lilac. All that remains of yesterday's Siamese are the sapphire-blue eyes and the mercurial disposition.

Many exhibitors advertise their cats and their catteries by placing signs on top of the cages—like this bold black-and-white sign that proclaims, "Turkish Van: The Cat who Loves Water." Inside the cage lolls a chalk-white cat, her plumed auburn tail swirled around her slim silken body. Auburn splotches the broad wedge head with prominent

Gotier Gigi, Siamese Lilac Point female—*BR/OW: Henri Pelletier & John Goterch, PH: Henri Pelletier.*

Lotsaluvan's Kizi Van Kedi, Turkish Van Auburn & White male—*BR/OW: Ann R. Van Brunt, PH: Mark McCullough.*

SGC Shirecats Coonsbarrie Dann, Maine Coon Brown Classic Tabby neuter: OW: *Michael & Elizabeth Bannenberger, BR: Todd & Cheri Glosier, PH: Olin Mills.*

cheekbones, a long nose, and large round eyes. The reference to water is factual: in Turkey it is not unusual to see a Van pleasure-swimming in a lake or a river.

In Ring 3 longhair adults are competing. A full-chested male, towering on powerful legs, fills one of the cages. Tufted ears twitching, he stares at his admiring audience.

Size is one of the attractive features of the *Maine Coon*. Males average 18 to 22 pounds. Although the coat is long and shaggy, a sparsity of undercoat makes it manageable. Gentle and loving, the Maine Coon is excellent with children and shows an almost doglike devotion to family.

Gracing the judge's table is another longhair from Turkey. Highly intelligent, the *Turkish Angora* readily learns simple tricks. This one is a male; his pure white coat, slim legs, dainty paws, and long feathered ears give him an air of aristocratic elegance. As with many white cats, Angoras are prone to deafness, especially the "odd-eyed" like this one, with one eye gold and the other blue.

It's well past noon and the pudgy judge in Ring 4 wipes his beaded brow and glances longingly at a food booth. He has one more longhair

Angelique, Chinchilla Persian female kitten – OW/PH: *Denise Foster.*

to consider, a female *Chinchilla Persian.* As he places her on the platform, the spectators murmur and crane their necks. Incredible coat! Flowing, luxuriant, every hair in place. With her short, thick legs, cobby body, luminous green eyes, and plumed tail, she's one of the real beauties of the exhibit.

At most cat shows the food concessions sell only sandwiches and drinks. No matter – a predawn breakfast can make a ham sandwich taste like ambrosia and an iced Coke the nectar of gods. This is a good time to mull over the cats seen thus far, including unusual breeds like the *Scottish Fold* with its envelope ears, the tailless *Manx,* and the hairless *Sphynx.* Another exotic shorthair, the high-cheekboned, tilt-eyed *Japanese Bobtail,* has a fascinating Oriental look. The delegation of silver-blue *Korats* from Thailand is delightful; unchanged for centuries, the Korat is still being used as a watch-animal in remote Thai villages.

Thus far it's been all adult cats. Which may seem odd, because a kitten is what most prospective buyers are seeking.

The evasion is deliberate. A baby, any kind of baby, is always adorable. But how can you know what she will be like when full grown?

GC Shadyshack's Rocky Road, Scottish Fold Silver Tabby w/White male—*BR/OW: Linda Rader, PH: Mark McCullough.*

Jinjerbred Purrsuede Me, Blue/White Sphynx male—*BR/OW: Sherry Jordan, PH: Tetsu Yamazaki.*

GC Choneko Kurisama Tenshi of Cyreccia, Japanese Bobtail Mi-ke female— BR: *Dee Hinkle & Elizabeth Funk, OW: Ray & Cherise Jolley, PH: Mark McCullough*

Korat on guard

If you're a novice, consider the adult cat first; she will be with you much longer than the kitten.

The loudspeaker abruptly booms "Allbreed Championship Finals in Ring 4!" Ignoring the noisy onrush of spectators, the rotund judge hunches over his scoresheets. As the numbers are called, the finalists, some holding their cats over their heads, make their way to the ring.

An air of expectancy hangs over the audience.

With a flourish, the judge places on his table a Bi-Color Persian, declaring it his tenth best cat. Ninth place goes to a Chocolate Point Siamese. The incredible Chinchilla Persian female takes eighth, and seventh goes to the Ruddy Male Abyssinian. A rascally Turkish Van swipes at the sixth place rosette to the amusement of the onlookers.

Considerable prestige is attached to the next five finalists. Fifth place is won by a Blue Cream Persian with deep copper eyes and a precisely halved blue-and-cream chin. A chunky Tortie Point Himalayan takes fourth. The third place rosette is awarded to a Tortoiseshell American Shorthair. Two Persians remain to compete for the title of Best Cat in Show.

It's a difficult decision. Both contestants are breathtaking. A wide silver ruff frames the jet-black face of the Smoke Persian male. His ear tufts are silvery, his top coat ebony shading to silver on the flanks. Round copper eyes enhance the full-moon face.

The Smoke's competition offers a striking contrast. Petite and dainty, her silken, lily-white coat sweeps the table. Eyes of cornflower blue, a delightfully turned-up nose, and a pouty mouth give her a piquant expression.

The judge names the White Persian female Second Best Cat in Show. A scattering of disappointed sighs can be heard. But applause for the winner is enthusiastic—apparently the Smoke male was the audience's favorite.

Selection of a Persian for Best Cat (or Kitten) seems to be the norm at most shows. Occasionally another breed wins, but this is the exception. Judges are required to base their awards on specific standards, but judges are human and can be swayed by personal opinions as to what constitutes the epitome of those standards. Some may lean to a particular breed or to certain patterns or colors. Some prefer longhairs to shorthairs, some like a sparkling personality, others a serene one. As the saying goes, beauty is in the eye of the beholder.

On the whole, however, judges are to be commended on their sincere attempts to rule impartially. Theirs is a tough job. Initial training is intensive and then they must go through a period of apprenticeship. Once approved as show judges, they endure long hours of standing on their feet and are subject to dark looks from disappointed exhibitors and occasionally painful injuries from the cats themselves.

Show catalogs may list kittens or cats for sale. Exhibitors often bring to a show their pet-class felines, seeking to place them in good homes. Be wary of inflated prices, and always ask for a health guarantee. Perhaps the biggest drawback to buying a kitten at a show is one's inability to visit and assess its parents and home environment.

If your objective is not a pet but a quality purebred, you won't find one for sale in a show hall. Such transactions do take place, but only among exhibitors. For the novice, a show offers a place to look and to learn, and once decisions are made, to use the valuable contacts afforded by such an exhibit.

Scanning the Market

Time of year has a significant effect on the cost and availability of a pedigreed kitten. Prices rise dramatically during the Christmas season because the supply cannot meet the demand. The best time to buy is late spring or early summer.

During this period, scores of pets-for-sale ads crowd the classifieds of newspapers. Why so many? No takers. People are relaxing, going on vacations, entertaining visitors. Some are moving, intent on getting resettled before school resumes. For the majority of would-be kitten buyers it's simply the wrong time of the year.

Meanwhile, all those furry bundles of energy from early spring matings await homes. Which means that a buyer can be selective because there are more to choose from. Breeders are so eager to sell that many will cut prices. This is not to imply that *every* breeder is itching for business; some will hold on to their kittens, hoping for a market upswing. Those who breed grand champions wouldn't even consider selling a quality female to a beginner.

Start your kitten quest by phoning the most promising of the classified ads. Check back with the cat fanciers you met at the shows. Contact breeders who advertise in cat magazines. Ask friends where they bought their cats. Talk to veterinarians' receptionists and clerks in pet stores. Check breeders' business cards on bulletin boards.

Whether it's a large registered cattery with a terrific reputation or an individual whose purebred is selectively mated once a year, consider carefully the kitten's environment. Is it clean? Odor free? Where are the cats kept? Are they cared for and loved? Is the breeder organized? Knowledgeable? Businesslike?

Deplorable conditions exist in some so-called "good" catteries. Run-down garages, old trailers, sheds, and other outbuildings hold cages crammed with cats. They lie in their own feces, fight for food, often breed indiscriminately. Rarely does a human hand touch them except to reprimand or to give shots or to hastily bathe when a prospective buyer looms on the horizon. Regardless of the ribbons and rosettes decorating the walls, you don't want to buy a kitten from this kind of environment.

Even worse conditions prevail in kitten mills. Most of these operate in the midwestern states and ship to pet dealers all over the country. As with the infamous puppy mills, the cats are stuffed into cages where they mate and bear their kittens in filthy conditions. The harvest of tiny lives is contracted for at minimal cost while the retailer foists exorbitant prices upon a gullible public.

The cost of a purebred cat or kitten from a reputable cattery is based on breed, quality, and pedigree. Exceptions can occur: time of year, as mentioned earlier, or circumstances of pressure, for example a breeder heavily overstocked or going out of business can affect price. In certain parts of the country, particularly rural, one may be forced to sell at a lower price. Generally, females are costlier than males; so are cats sold with papers. The age of a cat is also relevant, as is its physical condition and breeding ability.

A kitten eight to twelve weeks of age adapts quickly to a new environment. An older kitten or an adult require more time. Still, one might want to consider a half-grown kitten or a young adult. She's had all the baby ailments, been fully immunized, her general appearance is established, and—a big plus—she can be bred sooner.

Whatever the age or the price, the kitten should meet certain requirements. She should be fully weaned, box-trained, and parasite-free. Preferably, she will have been examined by a veterinarian, been given at least the first of her kitten immunizations, and been tested for FIP (Feline Infectious Peritonitis) and FeLV (Feline Leukemia Virus).

Her papers should include a *health certificate,* a *pedigree* going back four generations, a *registration* slip from one or more national cat registries, and an *agreement of sale.*

Even with all this, you can't be too careful. Examine the kitten personally. Sniff her breath for sourness. Peer under her tail for signs of worms or diarrhea. Feel her limbs for nodes. Look for a healthy pink mouth. Clean even baby teeth. Bright eyes with no wet discharge. Ears free of black crusty debris (mites). A lustrous coat with no bare patches.

Spend some time watching the kittens at play. Note the aggressive one, the crybaby, the sulker. Don't be captivated by the waddly little butterball—that cute plumpness may be a sign of bloat or parasites. Steel your heart against the sweet kitten with the slight limp—the adorable runt—the shy creature huddled in a corner.

Select a kitten with a well-proportioned body, not too large, not too small—one who is friendly, who does not skitter away from you or struggle when you try to hold her. If she purrs, great! But don't expect to be greeted immediately. Cats, even tiny ones, are cautious by nature, thoroughly inspecting a stranger before acceptance.

The possibility always exists that a kitten will choose *you.* I recall an occasion when a young couple had already selected their Himmie when another furry baby settled itself on the wife's lap. "Oh, look! It likes me!" was her delighted exclamation, soon to be followed by, "Don't you think we should adopt this one instead?"

They did, and it remained for the first kitten to wait until Her Persons arrived.

Feline Economics

Purchasing a purebred female can be expensive, often more so than budgeted. Novices tend to go ahead anyway, believing that their original investment will be repaid when they sell their first litter. Some even think that the kittens will earn them a profit.

Wrong. Breeders who realize a profit number in the minority. For most of us it's all we can do to break even. Veterinarian fees constitute the biggest expense. Depending on the area, the doctor, and the general health of the kitten, doling out $300 to $500 for first-year maintenance is not unusual. Why so much? Immunizations, tests, worming, baby illnesses, medications, vitamins, teeth-cleaning—the list can go on and on.

Breeding isn't cheap either. There's the stud service fee, prenatal care, special tests, special vitamins, special food, possible pregnancy problems or delivery mishaps, and postnatal care. When the kittens are eight or nine weeks old, it's their turn to put the bite on the breeder. Before being sold, each kitten needs a physical examination and at least a first "baby" immunization. If problems are found, the bite goes deeper. Mind you, these are only health care costs. Registration, advertising, food, litter, and grooming and furnishing items remain, as well as those unforeseen expenses that pop up when you can least afford them.

Seasoned breeders will usually immunize their own cats and kittens. Taking on the role of a vet, however, can involve risks. I remember a kitten who three weeks after I brought him home came down with a severe respiratory ailment. The breeder I bought him from had assured me that he was fully immunized. He was—but according to my vet, with inadequate vaccines.

If funds are low, you can use the pet clinics that give immunizations at a reduced cost. Or you could attend a class on animal husbandry to learn the basics. Whatever you decide, keep in mind that a prospect is more inclined to buy when proof is given that a kitten has been vet-checked and vet-immunized.

Breeders who have been in the business long enough to produce grand champions can, and usually do, make money. For the rest of us, it's encouraging to note that eventually there might be a *little* material gain. Most of the time, though, what comes in goes right out again for simple maintenance.

It's always been my belief that a breeder's greatest return comes from the intangibles—the pride and satisfaction enjoyed from the breeding of beautiful, healthy animals, and an appreciation of the role one plays in the lives of others. The kitten you breed may be the baby a childless couple long for, a buddy to a lonely boy, or solace for a widow. Contacts made through your cats will broaden your horizons and enable you to reap a rich harvest of friends.

Kittenizing the Home

Your first obligation to your new kitten is her safety.

Before bringing her home, make a thorough inspection of the premises. Put out of paw's reach such things as plastic bags, cleaning products, cigarettes, matches, yarn, rubber bands, candles, and fragile decorative objects. Check closures on doors and windows, closets, cupboards, and drawers. If there is a fireplace, close the flue, clean out the ashes, and block it.

Electrical cords should be wrapped in protectors; feline babies love to use cords for teething rings. Cover outlets with safety plug inserts.

Remove or place high all houseplants, real or plastic; plastic can be as toxic as parts of living plants. (See Appendix #9 for a list of toxic plants.)

Search for buttons, pins, needles, coins, bobby pins, string—all those little tidbits kittens love to chew on or tote around in their mouths.

Start now to always drop the toilet lid, to check the refrigerator before closing the door, the washer and dryer before operating.

If your home has an upper deck or if you live in a high rise, keep doors and windows locked. Your kitten may be blessed with the proverbial nine lives, but you don't want her losing the first one via a plunge from the sundeck.

Layette For a Feline Baby

The prospective kitten-parent will shop pet stores just as the prospective human-parent shops baby stores. Both may be inclined to dismay at the high cost of bare essentials.

Try the large chain pet stores for lower prices. Another alternative is merchandise offered at yard sales and swap meets, which usually only needs laundering or disinfecting. One can also take advantage of the excellent discounts given by mail-order pet catalogs. Vendors at cat shows offer the latest in feline equipment at reasonable prices.

In case you're uncertain as to what comprises a feline layette, here is a check list:

Bed (opt.): A shaped foam rubber or polystyrene bed with a washable cover is warm, lightweight, and comfortable. That cozy-looking wicker or rattan basket will harbor flea eggs, be difficult to clean, and present a hazard to a teething kitten. A wide variety of beds tempt the new cat owner—hammocks, igloos, boots, beanbags, heated beds. Take your pick. Your kitten will take hers, most likely your satin-covered pillow.

Cat carrier: To bring her home in and for trips to the vet or a show. Lightweight plastic or fiberglass is best; make sure it's well-ventilated, escape-proof, and large enough to allow for growth.

Cleaning aids: Pine products can be toxic. Safe cleaners are listed under Tips.

Dishes: Preferably glass, ceramic, or stainless steel. Plastic can cause chin acne. Cats dislike soiling their whiskers, so a low round bowl is a good choice. Bowls set into holders are excellent for water or dry food; they prevent spills and eliminate the need for the cat to stoop. Set food and water containers on a mat a distance away from the litter box.

Food: Initially what the breeder advises. Diet will be discussed in a future chapter.

Food supplements: Also in that future chapter.

Grooming tools: A brush and a comb suitable for the length of your kitten's hair, a flea comb, cotton balls, cotton swabs, and a nail cutter.

Litter box: The usual plastic type will do. Be sure it's wide enough not to tip and deep enough to thwart feline attempts to make a sand-pile beside it. A variety of box fillers and scoops are available. (See Tips.)

Medicine chest: Make this a well-labeled, lidded box. Include in its contents:

Blunt-tipped *scissors* such as used for infants' nails.

Hydrogen peroxide. A multi-purpose product. Diluted with water, it effectively cleans blood, food, or saliva from fur. Mixed with a small amount of baking soda, it makes a good cat toothpaste. It can serve as an emetic to induce vomiting and as a disinfectant for cuts and scratches.

Kaopectate (opt.) for simple diarrhea.

Laxatone, Petromalt, or a similar preparation for use as a lubricant to eliminate hairballs. Also used as a mild laxative.

Medicine dropper (opt.). Plastic, *not* glass.

Nutrical (opt.). A high calorie supplement to stimulate appetite and supply nutrition to an ill or recuperating kitten.

Rectal thermometer and a lubricant such as Vaseline.

Tweezers to remove splinters or glass.

Prescribed medications.

Scratching post: To exercise and tone a kitten's muscles, as well as a furniture-drapery-and-sanity-saver for her owner! The base should be broad and heavy to keep the post from tipping. Numerous sizes, styles, and coverings glut the market. Coverings vary from rope, burlap, and low-pile carpet to plain bark. Cats seem to prefer a rough, scratchy texture like sisal. Catnip-scent to entice.

Toys (opt.): Balls, catnip mice, a feather, peacock feathers, fabric toys — examine each for safety and durability.

Water: A change in water can be upsetting for a young kitten. Get a container of water from the breeder and mix it with yours. Gradually use less of the borrowed water. Freshen daily and always wash the bowl in soap and hot water.

Another way to cut the cost of a kitten layette is making do with items already at hand.

Bed: Fashion one from a cardboard box with high sides. Cut the front low enough to allow entry and line with towels or a small blanket. A large plastic dishpan, plumped with a small, towel-covered pillow, also makes a cozy bed.

Cord covers: To foil that insistent chewer, rub the length of the (unplugged) cord with pure vinegar.

In lieu of electrical plug inserts, tape plastic wrap over the outlets.

Files: A loose-leaf notebook with plastic-covered pages will serve to record such things as kitten sales, stud services, immunizations, data on other breeders, prospective buyers, etc.

Grooming: Substitute a used natural bristle hairbrush for that expensive cat brush.

Litter box: The standard 11 × 13 plastic dishpan will suffice if the sides are not too high. A slotted metal spoon makes an excellent scoop.

Scratching post: Assemble from wood scraps. Cover with carpet remnants from a yard sale.

Toys: They don't have to come from a pet shop. Try these ideas:

Twist a large pipe cleaner or several plastic straws into an intriguing shape and skid it across the floor.

Toss into a bathtub a pingpong ball or a corn cob, a plastic hair curler, anything that can be batted around to make an exciting noise.

Give your kitten a ringside seat to bird-watching by hanging a feeder outside her window perch.

Blow soap bubbles for her to catch. Let her leap or peep through doors and windows cut into large cardboard boxes.

Roll and tape together a carpet remnant to make a super tunnel for running through, jumping on, and hiding in.

Take your kitten fishing by fastening a stuffed mouse to a cord attached to a stick or a fishing rod.

A cardboard tube from toilet paper or plastic wrap makes a good roll-arounder, as does a fishing bobber or a round wooden clothespin.

Drop into an empty prescription bottle a little dry cat food. Then put on the cap and watch your kitten rock 'n' roll.

More fun toys: An empty oatmeal box. Plastic haircurlers or buttons hung on a cord. Empty shoe or tissue boxes. Dixie cups. Wads of foil. A plastic ring from a gallon milk jug.

Dip any toy in catnip for added excitement.

When assembling a kitten's equipment, use your imagination. The dollars saved could pay for her first stud service.

American Bobtail Brown Tabby Kitten—
BR/OW/PH: *Lisa Black*

2
THE FIRST YEAR

Adjusting

Coming abruptly into a strange environment can be a traumatic experience for a kitten. Make the first day or two quiet and without visitors. Keep her in her own room and be with her as much as possible. This will prove mutually beneficial. Your kitten will have an opportunity to become familiar with her new surroundings. Because of your presence, her anxieties will ease. To your advantage, you can observe her eating, drinking, and elimination habits. And you won't have to chase her from room to room or panic if she can't be found.

Once she has settled in, let her discover the rest of her new home by *carrying* her about. Put her down in each room and allow her to investigate the area before you move on. Cats have nine senses—smell, touch, sight, hearing, taste, balance, direction, temperature, and time. Your kitten will use most if not all of them in acclimating her small self to this big new world.

That first day feed her lightly. She may not eat much anyway, being too nervous or too busy exploring. After she eats, put her in her litter box and encourage her to eliminate. When she does, praise her.

It goes without saying that you'll want to take your new baby to bed with you. *Don't.* It establishes a habit difficult to break and a time may come when circumstances will force you to break it.

Settle the kitten for the night in her own room. Give her a stuffed animal to cuddle with. An alarm clock could be comforting, its ticking reminiscent of her mother's heartbeat. If you're still having qualms about leaving her alone, turn on some soft music or a night light.

Of course if your kitten's room is also your bedroom, you'll have no alternative but to accept her as a sleep-partner. Which of us has the heart to push from our pillow a tiny bundle of throbbing contentment?

One more thought. Because cats intensely dislike change, try to make every day similar to the one preceding it. As your kitten acclimates, life will settle into a routine. You'll learn to live with her little idiosyncrasies and she with yours.

Kids and Kittens

If young children are in the home, they should be instructed in the care and handling of a small pet.

Using a stuffed animal as a substitute, show the child how to pick up a kitten by placing one hand on the chest behind the front legs and the other under the hindquarters. Then demonstrate how to scoop it up and, still supporting its rear, cradle it close to the body. Caution very young children to always sit on the floor when holding a kitten.

Give rules to youngsters, and make the reason for such rules clear. If they indulge in rough play or wild running, the kitten could get stepped on. Teach the importance of keeping doors closed by describing the outside dangers that a kitten could face should someone be careless. Tell them how sensitive a cat's ears are to loud music or shrill screaming. Give them strict "no" rules—no poking, pinching, kicking, pulling the tail, or hugging too hard—it hurts! A kitten needs food and rest just as children do, so do not disturb her when she is eating or sleeping.

Never leave a child under six years of age alone with a kitten. Either of them could be injured.

These admonitions do not mean that children can't share in the nurturing of the new family member. Let them take part in her grooming and feeding. Give them individual cuddle and play times with her; supervised contacts are excellent for human and feline small-fry alike.

As the kitten grows, she will be better able to protect herself. The children will have learned to comply with the rules, and the novelty of a new pet will have worn off.

Grooming and Bathing

Avoid the trauma of a bath the first week or even the first month unless your kitten is in dire need of it. Which is unlikely—feline saliva contains a detergent as well as a deodorant. Your kitten has her own hairbrush, her tongue, which is covered with hard flexible spines. She has her own comb, her incisor teeth—although small, they can nibble off bits of grit, dry skin flakes, and even comb through small mats. Her front paws are her washcloth. When her hairbrush tongue or her comb teeth can't reach a certain part of her body, she wets her washcloth paw with her soap saliva, and scrubs.

A kitten is groomed much oftener than bathed. Longhairs require grooming daily. Shorthairs can get by with every other day grooming.

To avoid backaches, be sure the grooming table or counter is the right height for you. Slip on an apron and have ready your tools—brush, combs, cotton balls, cotton swabs, and the like. Briefly cuddle your kitten to relax her before placing her on the table.

No specific order is called for, but generally the ears are done first.

Lightly dampen a cotton ball or a swab with mineral or baby oil. Wipe only the *inside surface* of the ear, taking care to swab all the creases —never poke anything into the ear opening. Once a week is sufficient for kittens; their ears seldom have the oily residue prevalent in older cats.

Small gritty "sleepers" in inner eye corners can be cleaned with cotton balls moistened in a mild boric acid solution. Cotton balls can also be used for *tearing*, an unsightly dark stain that occurs in short-nosed breeds such as Persians and Himalayans. For stubborn eye corner stains try one of the commercial tear stain removers.

Occasionally wipe the paw pads with a soft moist cloth and check between them for cuts or foreign objects.

When grooming longhairs, some breeders comb the coat first. I prefer brushing, which not only relaxes the recipient but helps remove snarls. After brushing, use a wide-toothed comb on the body fur, and with short strokes comb against the grain, a section at a time. For those pesky mats lying close to the skin, try a seam ripper *carefully* or work in a commercial product such as Ring 5 Untangle.

Smooth facial hair with a small moist toothbrush. Wipe the coat with a damp cloth to remove loose hairs and dander; then fluff.

Occasionally a longhair will have feces stuck to its "pantaloons." Unless a kitten is being shown, keep this area trimmed.

Cat being brushed.

For shorthairs use a fine-toothed comb, a slicker brush, or a grooming mitt. Employ *downward* strokes from head to tail tip. Final-polish the coat with a piece of silk or a chamois.

Longhair or shorthair, keep in mind the sensitive parts of the feline body – the tail, the rump, the inner thighs, and the stomach. Groom with slow, gentle movements. If resentment is shown, either stop or shift the action to more pleasurable areas like the neck and the throat.

Teeth cleaning is a part of grooming that is often overlooked. Scrape tartar from teeth with your thumbnail, a small spoon, or a coarse cloth. To brush, use a child's toothbrush dipped in a solution of ½ teaspoon of salt to a cup of water. Fade tartar stains by rubbing teeth with a coarse cloth dampened in hydrogen peroxide.

To save furnishings and for your own and your kitten's comfort, clip the claws every two or three weeks. The front paws each have five claws, the back paws four. Begin with the front; press on the large paw pad to make the claw extend. Using a small nail clipper or one expressly for cats, trim the *tip*. Avoid the tiny vein (the quick) running through each claw; it will bleed if cut. Keep styptic at hand to stop bleeding in case of a mishap.

Nail clipping is easier if another party holds the kitten during the procedure. If your feline starts fussing, stop and do the rest later.

A cat is bathed to remove dirt and oils, dispose of a flea problem, or prepare for a show. My cats are bathed in the kitchen sink except for a big male who gets his scrub in the tub.

Early afternoon is the best time; the air has warmed and enough hours remain for the coat to dry. Make sure windows and doors are closed and the room is warm. Place within easy reach the bath tools: towels, bath brush, cotton balls, Vaseline, and a squeeze bottle of cat shampoo diluted half and half with warm water. Diluted shampoo penetrates better and rinses more easily.

Protect the floor with plastic. Put something in the sink for your kitten to stand on, like a heavy towel, an old bath mat, or a piece of screening. Fasten your plastic apron. Attach the sprayer to the tap. Mix hot and cold water to a comfortable temperature; test on your wrist.

Place your kitten on the countertop. Put a dab of Vaseline above her eyes and, if you wish, cotton balls in the ears. Earlier you will have trimmed her nails and thoroughly brushed her coat to remove any mats.

Use a damp terry cloth to moisten her face, then wash gently with a *tiny* amount of Baby Tears Shampoo on a toothbrush. Have a little water in the sink to wet the washcloth for thorough face rinsing.

Turn on the tap; it should take only a few seconds for the water to become temperature safe. Stand your kitten in the sink, facing *away* from you. Keep a firm grip with one hand while with the other you hold the spray. Bring it close to her body to soften the noise. It's the *sound* of water that alarms cats.

If your kitten simply will not tolerate a spray, try partly filling the sink with warm water and slowly immersing her. Use a sponge or a diaper to soak the coat. If she continues to behave wildly, hold her by the scruff of the neck; this usually freezes a cat.

After thoroughly soaking the fur, turn off the water. Apply the diluted shampoo, starting with a small amount on the head. Work around the neck into the ruff, the back, and the stomach, adding shampoo as you proceed. Lather; then use the brush, scrubbing first in one direction, then the other. Give special attention to the tail, the crooks of the legs, the paw pads, and behind the ears.

Check water temperature, then rinse. Do a thorough job, removing every trace of shampoo. If another soaping is necessary, follow the same procedure.

As a final rinse some breeders use one tablespoon of white vinegar to one quart of warm water, pour it over the coat, rub it in, and then rinse with clear water.

For that bath-fearful kitten, do not use the spray to rinse; instead, immerse her a number of times in clean warm water. Emptying and refilling the sink can be a tedious process, but in this instance it's a necessary one.

Press as much water from the fur as possible. Place the kitten on a towel. Use several towels to dry, employing a blotting motion rather than brisk rubbing, which tends to snarl the coat.

To dry, use a handheld blow-dryer set on low temperature. When partly dry, start brushing the fur up and out. If your kitten panics at the noise of a hair dryer, put her in a cage or a carrier and dry the coat by means of a small space heater with a blower.

Rascals and Angels

Behavior. With kittens it's erratic. It's like the old nursery rhyme: "When she was good, she was very, very good. When she was bad, she was horrid." Not that your feline baby could ever be horrid, heaven forbid! She's bound to be stubborn, though, and persistent. She'll dream up more ways of making mischief than you thought existed. Which is perfectly normal; if her behavior were always perfect, she wouldn't be feline.

A cat-owner, like a child's parent, can put up with personality quirks or use discipline. No matter how small the kitten, she needs to be taught house rules. Praise her when she's good. When she's naughty, reprimand. Not with a slap or a kick; never use physical punishment. A light swat with a newspaper won't hurt her, nor will a shower from a spray bottle. If worse comes to worst, take her to her room and shut her in.

Here are some typical behavior problems, their probable causes, and feasible ways to correct them:

Avoiding grooming: This may go back to an unpleasant grooming episode, or possibly yours is one of those cats who dislikes restraint. Give her a favorite dry food to nibble during grooming or pause to offer a special treat. Try grooming when she is drowsy; a sleepy kitten is usually tractable.

Be firm about grooming; it prevents your kitten from swallowing large amounts of fur and keeps your home and your person comparatively free of annoying hair.

Bats in the belfry: Racing around the house, leaping on furniture, bouncing sideways stifflegged, fur puffed and back arched, does not mean that your kitten is having a fit. It's an explosion of energy—she feels so good that she doesn't know what to do with herself. This often happens in the evening after sleeping all day. Catnip or too much rough play may also cause outbursts. The best cure is to let her run it out. Eventually she will tire. If you are afraid she might hurt herself, try spraying her with water, or turn out the lights.

Biting: A kitten may bite accidentally while playing or she may be pretending that you are her prey. She may resent being touched in certain places like the stomach or the base of the tail. Nips on the fingers, or "love bites," usually follow a period of stroking or grooming. These can also be hurting "passion bites," especially with a whole male, aroused by too lengthy a session of petting.

If an adult cat (particularly a male) clamps onto your hand, hold very still and offer no resistance. When released, back away slowly.

"Crazy cat!"

If the biter is a kitten, sharply snap its nose with your thumb and forefinger.

Clawing furniture, carpeting: Cats rarely claw to be spiteful; they have "legitimate" reasons. For instance, nature tells them that the flakey sheaths covering new claws need to be removed. What better way than raking them through the upholstery? Clawing is also comforting, a pleasant remembrance of pushing paws against mother's milk-laden breasts. In addition, it puts down a wonderful scent mark.

When your kitten starts clawing, shout *No!* and take her immediately to the scratching post. Or try covering the furniture with plastic—cats hate the feel of plastic. Keep nails closely trimmed.

Climbing legs: Maybe your kitten sees your leg as a cat tree? More likely, though, she is irritably demanding attention.

When your kitten jumps out at you or starts climbing your leg, grab her and tap her *hard* on the nose. Repeat four or five times, while scolding loudly.

Eating litter: Almost every small kitten chomps on litter. This generally occurs at four to five weeks of age, about the time milk teeth come in. Perhaps it feels good to sore gums. Or maybe it's that age when out of pure curiosity, everything has to be tasted.

About all one can do is remove kitten from box, litter from mouth, then try to distract with food or a toy. Or temporarily substitute shredded newspaper as a box filler.

Eating plants: You were supposed to remove them, remember?

Your kitten may have a craving for greens, which give her the folic acid absent in meat. Or she may have a hairball and instinct tells her that the greens will act as an emetic to expel it. Grow grass for her in a small container; kitty seed packets are available in most pet stores.

Excessive grooming: Grooming is a multipurpose activity. When a cat is bored, it grooms. When a cat is embarrassed, it grooms. After mating, it grooms. Before, during, and after kitten delivery, it grooms. During the heat of the summer, the saliva on a cat's fur acts like sweat does on human skin, becoming a kind of evaporative cooling system. Certain skin glands whose secretions keep the fur waterproofed are stimulated by grooming. Grooming removes the smell of humans and other odors that might be repulsive.

If licking becomes excessive and causes sores or bare spots, try to discourage with toys, food, or catnip.

Jumping on counters, tables: Cats like high places; they feel secure when they can look down on the world. Cats enjoy exercise; leaping is one form of stretching and strengthening muscles. Curiosity may draw them. Also, the smart cats know that their food is prepared on a counter or table.

Try a spray bottle of water. Bang on a metal pan. Shake a can containing gravel or marbles. Simply close the door to that particular room.

Pawing at food: This may be a throwback to life in the wild when felines buried the remains of their prey. Or maybe your kitten is not hungry or she doesn't like her food and is showing her distaste by trying to bury it.

Remove food, cover and refrigerate. Try later.

Refusing pills: A natural reaction; she feels lousy, and here you are trying to stick down her throat a strange, hard object.

Stroke the throat to encourage swallowing. If this does not work, crush the pill and put into butter or Nutrical. If she still refuses to swallow, rub the mixture into her paw; her penchant for cleanliness may make her lick it off.

Scratching: Again, this could be accidental during play. Or your kitten is defensive about a certain part of her body. Musky perfume, also, has a tendency to offend or to stimulate cats. To discourage, grip the front legs with one hand and with the other gently rub the tops of her paws. Talk to her in a soft, soothing voice until the claws retract.

Urinating, defecating outside the box: This is the most difficult bad habit to correct because of its variety of causes.

Check first with your vet for a physical problem such as parasites, constipation, impacted anal glands, diabetes, or a urinary tract infection. If the physical is ruled out, consider the emotional.

Cats are extremely sensitive to change. Has something new been brought into the home, like a baby, another pet, a different spouse, new furniture? Have you been preoccupied or busier than usual? Have you lately hosted house guests with small, noisy children? Has a family member or another pet recently died? Anger, jealousy, apprehension, loneliness, grief—any negative emotion can trigger a negative reaction.

A third cause of indiscreet elimination could be the facilities. All cats require privacy, a clean box, and enough room to comfortably squat. Some dislike highly perfumed litter and others object to liners. A cat may prefer two boxes, side by side, one for liquid waste, one for solids. Some want their boxes open; others prefer them covered. Placement is also important; the box should be out of traffic lanes and always in the same spot.

Correcting bad elimination habits takes time, work, and persistence. Measures like these may help:

1. Isolate the culprit, along with her box, food, and water, for a period of several days to several weeks. Allow her out for brief periods, which may gradually be lengthened. If she misbehaves, back she goes.

2. After cleaning and thoroughly deodorizing the soiled area, rearrange the furniture to cover it.

3. Spread aluminum foil where a cat has urinated. Place her food dish on it. Or try a fine spray of cologne on the area.

4. If a shower or a tub are favorite places, leave several inches of water in them.

5. Give catnip several times a week to help her relax.

6. If all else fails, your vet may decide to use a tranquilizer or a hormonal treatment.

Occasionally a female in heavy heat will urinate or spray due to physical pressure and psychological frustration. Almost always this stops once she is bred or out of season.

Spraying is altogether different from urinating and leaves a much fouler smell. To spray, a cat (usually a whole male) will back up to an object, lift the tail, and let go. Spraying is a feral behavior to mark territory. Some vets prescribe Ovaban for male cats with this habit; caution is indicated, because the drug can have strong side effects.

If a male is to be a pet only it's best to neuter him before puberty, which usually occurs at six to eight months. Generally speaking, whole males need to be confined in separate quarters.

Cats cannot be dominated, but they can be taught house rules. Make it clear what you want from your kitten. Then be insistent and persistent.

Fortunately, the negative facets of the feline personality are far outweighed by the positive ones.

No matter what age she is, a cat still thinks she's a kitten. Like Peter Pan, she will never grow up. She will always be a kitten and her owner will always be her mother, existing solely to love her and care for her. This is one reason why she likes being stroked. Her feline mother stroked her, in a different way but conveying the same tender message.

Touch is a cat's main source of affection. Every hair on the feline body has nerves that stimulate the brain to react. If the hairs signal that a touch is hurting them, the reaction is anger. If the touch is gentle, up goes the tail, the back arches, the eyes close, and deep-throated rumbles thank the pleasure-giver.

Your cat may demonstrate her love for you by rubbing against some part of your body. In thus marking you, she passionately announces, *This is My Person!* Additionally, the marking is an acceptance gesture; you are allowed into her life and into the world of cats.

Whiskers are very important sensory organs. If you cat condescends to touch your skin with her whiskers, ignore the tickle and enjoy.

If she head-butts you, feel flattered beyond words—head-butts are the ultimate expression of love.

Some cats lick. If yours decides to wash you, accept. You're not only her mother, you're her best friend. You've seen cats groom one

Exotic Shorthair Kitten, Silver Classic Tabby—BR/PH: Paul/Anna-Mae Bookbinder, Cakebread Exotics.

another; it's a mark of friendly affection. Not that it's necessary for you to reciprocate in the same manner!

Some cats hug. Not very many, but once in a while you'll be fortunate enough to have a hugger. Sita is my hugger. Whenever I pick her up, she slides her front legs around my neck and nestles her head against my cheek. It's a warm feeling to have a cat hug you.

Some cats kiss, usually on Their Persons' noses. Some tenderly pat the face. If your kitten adopts either of these habits, you have a for-life lover.

Some cats talk; feline talkers are usually Siamese or Himalayans. You may not understand much of the conversation, but you can sense that you're being given a great deal of attention. A soft, trilling sound means *Hi! I'm glad to see you!* It's similar to the chirruping noise with which a mother cat greets her kittens. The *Mom, I'm hungry!* announcement is usually a plaintive meow ending in a question mark.

Your cat may insist on being physically close to you, particularly when you are reading or trying to sleep. She may cling. She may nibble. She may tread against your chest. In her mind she is still a kitten and you are her mother and she needs to show you how much you are loved.

Then there's purring.

The mechanism of purring has always been something of a mystery. Various theories have been propounded as to what part of a cat's body the sound comes from. There's the premise that it is caused by a turbulence in the main blood vessel of the heart. Another opinion asserts

CH Lady Shalimar of Rajapur, Himalayan Lilac Point – BR: *Claire Brady, OW/PH: Elaine Gilbertson.*

that purring arises from vibrations of the soft palate. The most logical (and accepted) theory has it that purring originates in the feline voice box; by tensing its vocal cords, the cat causes a vibration each time it breathes in and out.

Cats have many kinds of purrs and each may mean something different. We tend to think of purring as an expression of pleasure and most of the time it is. But cats also purr when worried or frightened. Veterinarians often have to snap their feline patients on the nose to stop their purring so that chest examinations can be completed.

Queens in labor usually purr with feverish enthusiasm. Perhaps this outpouring of emotion is an expression of happiness, or it relaxes them (or maybe they do it to relax their human midwives!). Purring indicates contentment; before a kitten is a week old, it nestles into the warmth of its mother's body and purrs. Purring is a means of reassurance, as when a mother cat croons to her kittens. Or it is a way of comforting, as when a feline pet purrs to its Person when that Person is sad or upset. My Mitzee-Toi purred the night she lay dying in my arms, and I'll always believe that she sensed my grief and was trying to console me in the way she knew best.

Regardless of why or how, purring is the manner in which a cat communicates its deepest feelings to other cats or to humans. It is a subtle magic that weaves between giver and recipient a bond of peaceful togetherness.

3
HEALTH

Immunizations

Even though your kitten may have had all her "baby" immunizations, it is important that she be introduced to her veterinarian. A good animal doctor will check her weight and general health, and perhaps make dietary suggestions. That first visit will give kitten and vet an opportunity to become acquainted without the trauma of needle-sticking. In addition, she'll be on the office books as a patient.

The veterinarian is the second most important individual in your cat's life. I cannot stress enough the necessity of availing yourself of the services of a competent and caring small-animal doctor. Pet-owning friends and relatives, or perhaps the person from whom you bought your kitten may be able to refer you.

Not every kitten is fully immunized when it goes from the breeder to its new home; that responsibility is often left to the buyer.

Opinions vary as to how old a kitten should be for a first immunization. Some veterinarians say six weeks, some eight; others ten or twelve. Most agree, however, on a series of three injections spaced three weeks apart if begun *before* ten weeks of age. If begun *after* ten weeks, two injections are programmed.

Each injection holds four different vaccines. Vaccines contain viruses or bacteria that have either been weakened or killed so that when injected, they will not cause the disease. Your kitten reacts by producing antibodies to the specific agents in the vaccines. These "warrior" antibodies remain in the kitten's system for a certain number of months or years, affording protection from natural infections.

Perfect immunity is not yet attainable. Today's vaccines give slightly better than 95 percent immunity to the following diseases:

Feline chlamydiosis (pneumonitis): A respiratory disease caused by bacteria. Symptoms include eye infection, sneezing, coughing, and heavy salivation. The clinical signs of pneumonia are usually absent, but the lungs may still be involved. Kitten mortality rate is high.

Feline panleukopenia (distemper, cat fever, feline enteritis): An extremely contagious virus primarily affecting kittens, although cats of any age can become infected. The virus attacks various parts of the body, particularly the lymph nodes and intestines. High fever, vomiting, and weight loss are the first symptoms. Bloody diarrhea leads to dehydration and in most young kittens to death.

Feline rhinotracheitis and **calcivirus:** Two other respiratory diseases, the first being the most dangerous. Symptoms include fever, coughing, discharges from eyes and nose, and difficulty in breathing. Painful tongue blisters can keep the kitten from eating, resulting in dehydration. Treatment is difficult and lengthy. Cats that recover can become carriers.

These are the four most common feline diseases for which we have protection. Yearly boosters are imperative.

Feline leukemia virus (FeLV): This disease may one day be eradicated because we now have a vaccine. Usually transmitted by contact with an infected cat, FeLV attacks the immune system, leaving the body vulnerable to other diseases. Cats with FeLV almost always die of secondary infections such as anemia, pneumonia, or cancer. The first vaccine came out in 1984–85. Because it's so new, some cat owners are fearful of using it. The current vaccine is safe and rarely has side effects.

After a negative blood test, kittens ten to twelve weeks of age (some vets prefer older) receive two injections spaced three weeks apart. Yearly boosters are advised.

Feline infectious peritonitis (FIP): The year 1991 saw the acceptance of a vaccine for this usually fatal virus. No needle is used; the vaccine is administered in drop form, intranasally. Healthy cats, sixteen weeks or older, receive two doses spaced three to four weeks apart. Again, a yearly booster is recommended.

Rabies: This killed vaccine is usually given at twelve to sixteen weeks of age. It is of particular import if the pet is allowed outside.

Feline immunodeficiency virus (FIV): As of this writing, no vaccine is available for FIV, which is similar to human AIDS. Antibiotics and other drugs are used to treat infections and side-effects, but the virus itself is incurable. It should be noted that although FIV can be passed from one cat to another, it is *not* infectious to humans.

Today's vaccines rarely cause reactions, and if they do, they're usually minor—sleepiness, sore muscles, aches, sometimes a slight fever. Yet some of us hesitate about certain shots. A suggestion. If you are the worrying kind, make the vaccination appointment for early morning; thus, if an unfavorable reaction occurs, your vet would still be in his office.

Parasites

The healthiest of kittens can get parasites; some are even born with them. They are classified as either *internal* or *external*.

Internal Parasites
Coccidia
Cause: The eggs of these tiny, one-celled parasites are found in the feces of infected cats and are spread by ingestion.

Symptoms: Weight and appetite loss, diarrhea.

Remedy: Take a fecal sample to the vet, who will prescribe a treatment. If left untreated in young kittens, fatal debilitation may result.

Hookworms
Cause: May start from prenatal infections with the hookworm larva penetrating the fetuses in the womb. It can also come from the mother's milk or a kitten digging or eating around infected feces.

Symptoms: Pale gums, apathy, stunted growth, bloody diarrhea, or black, tarry feces.

Remedy: Take a fecal sample to your vet, who will prescribe pills or give an injection. Hookworms are the most dangerous internal parasite because they often cause severe anemia. Extreme cases call for iron treatments or blood transfusions.

Roundworms

Cause: Microscopic eggs on fur or food are ingested as the cat eats or grooms itself. Often kittens get roundworms from the mother's milk or while they are still in the womb.

Symptoms: Typically, a dull coat and potbelly. The worms resemble curled pieces of cream-colored spaghetti and may appear in feces or vomit.

Remedy: Take a fecal sample to your vet, who will prescribe accordingly. If left untreated, it can result in severe, sometimes fatal debilitation.

Tapeworms

Cause: Fleas (and rodents) carry tapeworm eggs. If a flea is accidentally eaten, the eggs absorb digested food within the intestine, then hatch into worms.

Symptoms: Classic sign is a ravenous appetite without weight gain. The kitten may drag its rear end on the floor to ease the itching. Tapeworms resemble white rice and are found in feces or clinging to the hair around the anus.

Remedy: Take in a fecal sample for analysis. An injection may be given or an easily administered pill called Droncet can be purchased from your vet.

These are the most common types of internal parasites. *Caution! Do not treat on your own.* Medication potent enough to kill these parasites could be deadly to a kitten if given in the wrong dosage or mixed with other medicines and chemicals.

Follow up all parasite treatments with another fecal analysis two or three weeks later to insure that the treatment has been successful.

External Parasites

Fleas

Fleas are bloodsuckers, worm carriers, and costly pests. In some parts of the country, fleas make a cat's life miserable throughout the entire year. A warm damp climate is conducive to egg-hatching, and one female flea can produce as many as 250,000 offspring in her lifetime.

Keeping your cat comfortable and your home livable entails work and expenditure. It is not enough to bathe or dip a cat; the environment must also be controlled. A professional exterminator can be hired or you can do it yourself. Foggers are effective, as are sprays and powder treatments; follow instructions exactly. Spray outside as well as inside areas—fleas can enter on clothing or shoes.

Other tactics include frequent flea-combing, twice-weekly laundering of cat bedding, and daily vacuuming. (See Tips for additional helps.)

Ear Mites

These can evolve into serious ear infections if not properly treated. Mites are readily detected by the dark, greasy residue in your kitten's ears and its annoyed scratching. To treat, first clean the ears with mineral oil or hydrogen peroxide. Dry thoroughly; then medicate with a vet's prescription. Also apply a small amount of medication to the tip of the tail; cats sleep with the tail tip curled next to an ear.

Since mites are highly contagious, every cat in the home should be treated.

Ringworm

Ringworm is not a worm, it is a fungus contracted by contact with an infected cat. It appears as a round bald spot, usually on a cat's ears, over the eyes, or down the front of the legs. The patches of fungi look dry and flaky and will often itch. On a longhaired cat, the fur in the contaminated area may need to be shaved in order to apply an anti-fungal cream. In some cases, special shampoos are used. An oral medication like Griseofulvin may be prescribed (but not for pregnant cats).

Other kinds of external parasites include head lice, ticks, and feline scabies. Your veterinarian will give instructions as to treatment.

Your kitten is relatively safe from external or internal parasites if sensible sanitary measures are employed and the pet is kept indoors.

Animal diseases to which humans are vulnerable are medically called *zoonitic* diseases.

Rabies is the most familiar. This usually fatal disease is transmitted to a human by a bite from a rabid animal.

Toxoplasmosis is another zoonitic disease. It can be transmitted to humans from a cat's feces. Because it is particularly dangerous to pregnant women, they should avoid handling a cat's excrement. Cats are not the only source of toxoplasmosis; raw meat also harbors the parasite, as do birds, mice, and other small animals. A simple fecal examination for parasites will identify most carriers.

Hookworms or *roundworms* can be passed to children playing in sandboxes or dirt areas where infected animals have dropped their feces.

Ringworm is highly contagious, as is the ringwormlike skin infection called *scabies*.

Cat scratch disease, which causes symptoms similar to that of influenza, can be transmitted from feline to human; so can *chlamydiosis*, which causes eye irritation and sneezing.

Certain individuals are highly allergic to flea bites.

It is unusual for a cat-owner to contract any of these diseases. They can easily be avoided by practicing good hygiene, keeping your pet inside the

home, and following a regular program of immunizations and veterinarian checkups.

Is My Kitten Sick?

Your kitten was born into an environment housing its own family of disease-causing bacteria. Due to the antibodies in her mother's milk, she remained immune to these germs. Now she has come into an entirely different environment, housing an entirely different bacterial family. She's healthy enough to avoid most ill effects but perhaps not all.

Within several weeks of entering a new home, some kittens become ill. Usually the ailment is minor. Listed below are a few common kitten complaints, along with guidelines for the worried cat-parent.

Appetite loss: Possible causes: overfeeding, warm weather, or loss of smell. Check nostrils for an impediment or a heavy discharge. If it continues, consult your vet.

Constipation: May be from insufficient water or food, not enough exercise, an unfamiliar litter box, or hairballs. Try a hairball preparation two or three times a day. Allow twenty-four hours before calling a vet. Do not give an enema unless it is ordered.

Coughing: If accompanied by gagging and spitting up, it usually means a hairball. Dose with Laxatone or a similar preparation *between meals* two to four times a week. If associated with runny eyes, sneezing, and phlegm, then it is a respiratory infection and needs prompt treatment.

Diarrhea: Possible causes: milk, stress, an infection, internal parasites, a change in diet. Try Kaopectate, ½ to 1 teaspoon every six to eight hours (a dropper is easiest to use). Give no food the first twenty-four hours but provide ample fresh water. The following day offer a bland diet of baby food meat or boiled chicken and rice. If looseness persists or fever and lethargy are present, notify your vet—a kitten can rapidly become dehydrated.

Frequent urination: Heat will temporarily make a kitten drink more water and consequently it will urinate more often. One must distinguish, however, between this kind of over-urinating and symptoms of FUS (Feline Urological Syndrome). FUS symptoms include: frequent box visits with irritable pawing, straining with little or no resulting flow, blood in the urine, drinking inordinate amounts of water, urinating outside the box, swelling of the abdomen. If any of these symptoms occur, get medical help immediately.

Panting: Your kitten is hot; cool her with a wet cloth. She may be distressed or fearful; soothe or distract. If panting continues, call vet.

Shivering or trembling: Could mean excitement or fear. One of my males always has a shivering episode when taken to the vet. Occasionally it signals an oncoming fever.

Vomiting: Possible causes: eating too fast, food too cold, swallowing some indigestible material such as grass or plastic. Most probable cause is a hairball. Give several doses of Laxatone or a similar preparation. Check food for freshness. Serve smaller portions and be sure food is at room temperature. Give ice cubes instead of water. If vomiting persists or if the kitten refuses food and becomes lethargic, call your vet. Vomiting kittens dehydrate even faster than kittens with diarrhea.

Most new kitten-owners, like most new parents, cherish the hope that their babies will always be well. Added to their worry is a fear of their own inadequacy.

Successful sick-kitten care depends on several factors. A good vet. The trust between a kitten and Its Person. Its Person knowing and performing the correct procedures.

The first step is to take your kitten's temperature.

Use a well-lubricated rectal thermometer and shake down below 100 degrees. Stand your kitten on a hard surface, preferably with someone holding her. If help is unavailable and the kitten is agitated, roll-wrap her in a large towel with the rump exposed.

Lift the tail and carefully insert the thermometer into the anus (top hole) just to the end of the silver. Leave in for at least one minute. Remove and wipe clean.

If your patient fights a rectal thermometer, take her temperature in the armpit just under the front leg, or in the groin, holding the hind legs snugly together for two or three minutes.

Normal feline temperature ranges from 100°F to 102.5°F. If above or below these numbers, contact your veterinarian promptly.

When medicating your kitten, protect your clothing with some sort of covering. As with temperature-taking, if help is unavailable, wrap the kitten in a towel before placing her on the counter.

With *liquid* medicine, use a syringe or a dropper instead of a spoon. Fill the syringe with the prescribed amount and insert it into the *side* of the mouth. Squeeze—a little at a time. Be careful not to pull her neck straight up but rather hold her jaw at an angle just high enough for the flow of gravity. Allow ample time to swallow.

Pilling is more difficult. After restraining your kitten, place one hand over the top of her head and get a firm grip on either side of her jaw. With the other hand, open the jaws. Quickly place the pill in the center of her mouth as far back over the "hump" in the tongue as possible. Close her mouth and hold firmly, as you tilt back her head and lightly rub her throat.

If she licks her nose, the pill has been swallowed. If she is stubborn and holds the pill in her mouth, try blowing gently in her face. Or if water is handy, put a couple of drops on her lips or nose tip—in licking, she will automatically swallow.

As a last resort, insert the pill into a favorite food. This rarely works, though, cats are too smart.

Your vet may prescribe a *skin medicine* for a fungus or dermatitis. Being naturally fastidious, your kitten may be inclined to lick off the foreign element. Foil this action by holding or playing with her immediately after rubbing in the ointment. Keep her distracted for ten or fifteen minutes so that the skin medication can dry or absorb.

Force-feeding is sometimes necessary with an ailing kitten. Wrap your patient in a towel with only her head exposed. Tip her head slightly

Cakebread's Muscatel,
Exotic Shorthair Kitten, Silver Patched
Tabby female —
BR/OW/PH: Paul
Bookbinder.

backwards and hold firmly — a kitten will shake its head to get rid of unwanted food.

If the food is a paste like Nutrical, squeeze a small amount into her mouth or on the roof of her mouth; if you can't get her mouth open, press the paste against her teeth. With liquid food or with water, use a syringe.

An ailing kitten must be kept warm and quiet. Sleep is an important adjunct to recovery; therefore, do not disturb unless absolutely necessary.

With all this talk of illnesses, immunizations, and parasites, new owners may start to wonder what they let themselves in for when they bought kittens.

If kept indoors and given the proper diet and medical care, most felines scamper through the years with very few problems. My Shahji enjoyed life relatively unscathed by illness until the ripe age of fifteen. At which time he decided he'd had enough, stopped eating, and soon afterwards went to sleep peacefully in his basket.

His last kittens were born three weeks after his death. Which demonstrates how healthy a cat can be if genetically sound and properly cared for.

Diet and Nutrition

Every cat food manufacturer is of the opinion that his particular researchers have come up with the perfect feline diet. From magazines to newspapers to television, grinning grimalkins peer from cans and boxes to proclaim the superiority of their product. The sheer number and variety of cat foods cramming supermarket shelves may overwhelm the novice.

It's not as bewildering as it seems.

The first few months present no problem; you feed your kitten the breeder-recommended diet. When the normal adolescent changes begin, diet modification is required. Your kitten's body will need more of the essential nutrients, in particular the B vitamins and the building blocks called proteins.

Cat owners try to meet these needs in a variety of ways. Some feed their cats raw meat. Some correlate cost with quality and buy only the most expensive food. A few huddle in their kitchens, concocting "secret" recipes. Your vet will recommend a scientifically formulated food, which is fine—if your cat likes it.

In point of fact, nothing is wrong with today's commercial foods. They're tasty, convenient, sanitarily packaged, and they provide all the nutrients needed. Three kinds predominate and each has its place in your cat's diet.

Canned foods contain proteins, fats, vitamins, minerals, and water. They're sterile, easy to store, and they smell and taste good to the feline palate.

Soft moist foods have similar qualities but are more expensive. They also contain sugar, and their protein and fat contents are lower.

Dry foods are the cheapest. They can safely be left out over a period of time and they help scrape tartar from teeth. Like soft moist, though, they have less protein and fat than canned. Because most are high in ash, they make the urine alkaline, thus having a tendency to cause urological problems.

When buying cat foods, study the labels. The number one feline need is *protein*. Meat is protein, so are fish, chicken, cheese, and internal organs like liver, heart, and kidney. Chicken is easily digested and it is high in taurine, an essential element for heart function, vision, and reproduction.

Egg yolk is another excellent protein source, but use with caution if concerned about the possibility of salmonella. See p. 142. Mix the egg yolk raw or cooked with other foods but no oftener than twice weekly.

In fact, don't overdo on *any* one type of protein. Too much liver can upset the bowels. A diet of only lean beef can develop into a debilitating lack of calcium and vitamins. An excess of tuna is the worst, causing a depletion of vitamin E, which results in nerve disease (steatis). Cat tuna also contains insoluble mineral salts that often form bladder stones or kidney stones.

Fats should constitute 25 to 30 percent of a cat's diet. Fats are found in meats. Or you can add to food ½ teaspoon of olive oil or melted butter. Daily amounts of fat give more energy and add luster to the coat and tastiness to meals.

Carbohydrates are not as vital as the other elements, but they provide a good source of energy, and their fiber stimulates proper elimination. Cereals are one source of carbohydrates.

All *vitamins* play an important role in nutrition, but certain ones supply the special needs of felines.

The multipurpose *vitamin A* assists in normal growth and protects against infections, toxic chemicals, and pollution. It helps ward off skin or eye problems. Liver is a natural source of vitamin A.

(Note: Because the urine does not excrete surplus vitamin A, supplement only on the advice of your veterinarian.)

B or *nerve vitamins* reduce stress, aid in metabolism, enrich the blood, and relieve skin problems. B vitamins are found in meat, liver, and green vegetables. Powdered brewer's yeast replaces those B vitamins that are destroyed by heat during the canning process.

Vitamin C is a natural urine acidifier. Add C to food by mixing in standard products like tomato juice, spaghetti sauce, or crushed C tablets.

Vitamin E promotes fertility. Cereals and some meats contain vitamin E.

Essential *minerals* include:
  Calcium for bones and teeth
  Chloride to keep body fluids balanced

Copper for forming hemoglobin
Iodine for proper thyroid function
Magnesium for the nervous system
Phosphorus for bones and teeth
Potassium for muscle development and function
Selenium for metabolism
Sodium, vital to kidney function
(Caution: too much potassium or selenium could result in FUS (Feline Urological Syndrome.)

What it all boils down to is *balance*. To promote health and vigor, feed a balanced diet of proteins, fats, minerals, vitamins, and water.

Of course your cat doesn't know that her food is "balanced," nor does she care. The only thing that's important to her is *does it taste good?*

Finicky eaters occur among cats the same as among other pets. Such pickiness may arise from being given the same food day after day. The solution is variety—in addition to the three types of commercial food, serve an occasional treat of fresh food. Boiled or baked chicken, and broiled or steamed fish make a welcome change. Use the juices to flavor dry food.

Be sure to remove all bones from meat and fish, and either mince or chop it; a cat's jaws are designed to move up and down, not sideways.

Occasionally treat your cat to other types of "people food." The taste buds of a human and a cat are very similar. Like us, they can differentiate between sweet and bitter, sour and salty. I've had cats who scorned liver for yogurt, who slurped with gusto cottage cheese and sour cream; cats who nibbled green beans and pizza and drooled over ice cream. The experts tell us that these foods are not good for cats. I agree—if they are fed nothing else. Like people, though, cats enjoy having their palates titillated once in a while.

No one seems to frown on catnip, but few people realize that catnip is a treatment as well as a treat. Not only is it an excellent source of vitamins A, B, and C, it soothes an upset stomach.

Two more thoughts regarding finicky felines.

Do you serve your cat food directly from the refrigerator? If so, that might account for her disdain. Cold hard lumps and congealed fats can be as repulsive to cats as to humans. Always serve food at room temperature or slightly warm it in the microwave.

Texture, too, may be a factor. Some cats like to chomp on lumpy food; others are partial to a smooth, creamy consistency. If the latter is your feline's preference, use a blender or a potato masher to prepare it. As to amount, two rounded tablespoons per feeding is sufficient for an adult cat, and for adults, two feedings per day is average.

The notion that milk is an integral part of a cat's diet is a fallacy. Milk causes diarrhea in most felines. If you insist on giving your cat milk, use evaporated and dilute with an equal amount of water.

Water is one of the essentials of a balanced diet. To encourage water drinking, try these ideas:

Add salt to food.
Place the water bowl a distance away from the food bowl.
Some cats hate to stoop; try a tall water container, like a wide-mouthed vase.
Stir into the water the juice from canned tuna or turkey.
Put a small rock or two into the bowl—your cat may like the flavor of leached minerals.

Because cats evolved as desert animals, they do not require as much water proportionately as do dogs or humans. Also, cats are able to conserve the water in their bodies by concentrating their urine.

4
BREEDING

Breeding Terms

A*queen* is a female cat with all her reproductive equipment intact. A *stud* or *tom* is a male cat similarly endowed. When sexual maturity is reached, the queen goes into a physical state commonly called *heat*, technically *in season* or *estrus*. After several such periods, the queen's sleep-starved owner decides to take her to a stud for the purpose of using her reproductive equipment in a function called *breeding*, *mating*, or *procreation*.

The *breeder* is the party who owns the queen at the time of mating. The queen is a *maiden* or virgin until she has been bred. The period of pregnancy is called *gestation*. Delivery of the kittens is *kittening*, *queening*, or *parturition*. To eliminate confusion, we'll use only "queening" and "parturition" in the chapters to follow.

The queen is now the *dam*, or mother, of a particular *litter* (group) of kittens. The stud is the *sire*, or father. The kittens are said to be *out* of the female and *by* the male (as Snowball *out* of Miss Trudie *by* Silent Sam).

Genetically, breeding can be categorized in four classes:

Inbreeding refers to matings between father and daughter, mother and son, sister and brother. Breeders of top show cats say that inbreeding is vital to maintain type, and it's true that many grand champions result from inbreeding. Inbreeding may bring out the best traits, but the catch is that it also may bring out the worst; faults such as kinked tails, crossed eyes, cleft palates, or deafness could emerge. For the novice, it's prudent to avoid inbreeding.

Linebreeding refers to the mating of cats who are related to a common ancestor such as a grandparent. Because it is not as close as inbreeding, the possibility of defects is lessened. So too is the possibility of getting a really high quality kitten.

Outcrossing constitutes the safest method for the beginner. Because neither sire nor dam have any relationship, new and strengthening bloodlines are brought in. The chance of genetic quirks is greatly reduced and the resulting kittens are usually larger and healthier. Type may not be as good, but there's always the chance that a quality kitten could crop up.

Crossbreeding refers to the breeding of two different breeds of cats. The Tonkinese emerged from the crossbreeding of Siamese to Burmese.

Estrus

Webster defines puberty as "the state of physical development when sexual reproduction first becomes possible." For female cats, this evolution occurs at six to eight months. As with everything feline, however, exceptions occur.

A first heat may flare slightly earlier or much later. The onset of estrus is influenced by a number of factors—genetics, nutrition, general health, environmental temperature, and especially the amount of exposure to daylight. A female born in late spring is not apt to start calling until midwinter of the following year. One born in the fall can roll into estrus as early as March. Experts claim that long periods of light stimulate feline hormonal activity. This could be why so few litters are born in winter and so many in spring and summer.

October through December is a quiet period for most cats. Comes January, though, and the atmosphere grows charged with awakening hormones.

About this time, veterinary offices ring up the curtain on their yearly spring drama. Switchboards are swamped with calls regarding cats going into fits, cats rolling in agony, cats moaning and howling all night long. Medical examination reveals that the alarming behavior is merely estrus. The stunned owner is apt to protest, "You gotta be wrong, Doc, she's only a baby! How can she possibly be in heat?" Having heard this a dozen times that day, the vet may be inclined to tartness. "She can and she is! For the next six months you can anticipate banshee toms, stinking stoops, and every time you open a door, little Maybelle here making a mad dash for freedom."

The vet may be stretching it a bit. Some queens go through only two or three seasons a year. On the other hand, some seem never to be out of heat. Siamese fit into the latter category; their shameless demands for their sexual rights appear never-ending.

If a queen is taken to be bred, estrus lasts three to five days. A successful breeding virtually guarantees the queen's owner a full nine weeks of blissful, uninterrupted slumber. If the female is *not* bred, her tortured midnight arias will continue for a ghastly ten days or even up to three weeks. Following which, a peaceful seven to fourteen days will prevail before her lusting hormones scream her back into heat.

Oddly enough, some owners appear oblivious to the fact that their queens are in season. This could occur because of a lack of mutual rapport, or perhaps the female is having a "silent heat." I had a queen named Ginger Blossom whose only sign of estrus was a slight decrease in appetite. She never rolled, she never called, never arched her back when stroked, or demanded excessive attention. The only way I could catch her was to keep a precise calendar on her estral cycles and when she was about due, pop her in with a stud.

Such behavior is rare. A cat owner would have to be blind, deaf, and dumb (*very* dumb) not to notice a queen in heat!

So how does one cope?

Reaction-action depends on temperament. If you're the patient type who for months has tolerated don't-touch-me! haughtiness, you're apt to go into ecstasies when Her Highness is transformed into a cuddlepuss. On the other hand, a tense individual could become unnerved at constantly being tailed by a longtail. Those of us whose days are work-crammed are apt to grow irritated at the constant demands for attention, and respond with a testy, "Shove off, cat!"

The best way to live with a sex-starved cat is to: a) love her and b) guard her. Usually she won't eat much, so tempt her palate with occasional treats. Talk to her and give her affection—stroke her head and throat but keep away from the lower back area where caressing could further arouse. When she squirms and moans, try distracting her with catnip or a new toy. Sometimes it helps to just carry her around the house.

Isolate her if she sprays, and especially if you're not home; frustration could affect her litter box habits. Unlike dogs, very few cats bleed during estrus; should yours chance to be one of them, this is another reason to keep her confined. Soft music, dim lights, or your voice on tape will help to ease loneliness.

Above all, be careful she doesn't slip outside. You won't believe how fast a cat in heat can move, or the number of sly tricks she can come up with to get to a waiting male.

If you don't plan on breeding your queen, by all means spay her (but *not* when she is in season). A cat who goes on and on in countless heats can become actually ill. Sometimes the uterus becomes painfully infected, leading to weight loss and apathy. Ovarian cysts can develop, producing unusual amounts of female hormones that may adversely affect her fertility.

Or it could go the other way, the body coping, but not the mind. Deprived females have been known to rub against objects until their faces actually bleed. Some paddle incessantly with their feet; some go through hours of postures simulating copulation; others pretend they've been mated and groom themselves to the point of making their flesh raw. Letting your queen go unbred for a few heat periods won't wreak any lasting damage, but depriving her for months and years could turn her into a neurotic, unhealthy cat.

If you intend to breed, consider first these vital issues.

Is your queen a year old yet?

Cats bred too young are more apt to miscarry or to require a C-section. They tend to have smaller litters and their kittens are sometimes puny or defective. An inadequate milk supply can be another problem. Often the young dam does not apply herself to the rearing of her young; still a kitten herself, she enjoys playing with her babies but ignores the demands of motherhood. Before breeding your queen, allow her to have at least three heats—this is nature's way of maturing the reproductive tract for future conception.

Is your queen up on her booster shots?

Pregnancy encompasses at least nine weeks; nursing another five or six. During this period, the female cannot be innoculated with a live vaccine because it might harm her kittens. She should be innoculated *before* breeding, not only for her own protection but to pass on immunity to her unborn kittens. The antibodies in her milk will later act as an additional safeguard.

Has your queen had a pre-mating checkup by a qualified veterinarian?

An adult female can appear perfectly well and still be carrying any-thing from a virus to ringworm. A fecal sample should be examined for parasites, in particular roundworms, which can deplete a pregnant female of proper nourishment and also be passed to kittens in the womb. Occasionally a throat or a nasal swab will be taken to study for viral or bacterial infections, or a blood test made to check for FeLV and FIP. Your veterinarian's sensitive fingers will probe for internal growths, lungs and heart will be listened to for rales or murmurs, anal glands expressed (squeezed) if necessary. Ruffling of fur will reveal any fleas, and an ear examination will show if there are mites. Weight, tem-perature, teeth, mouth and tongue color, eye clarity, reflexes—a good vet will run the gamut. When your queen gets that final OK, you'll know she's in prime condition to cope with the physical demands of being a mother.

What about the mental demands—is your queen's disposition suitable for motherhood?

Be honest. You've lived with your cat for a year or better, you know her psychological makeup. True, most felines are superb mothers, devoted, patient, loving. Once in a while, though, a queen does not fit the pattern. Extreme youth could be a factor, as previously men-tioned. Occasionally a cat is too lazy for the amount of work that motherhood entails, and she will expect *you* to take care of kitten chores. Or she may be the possessive type, jealous of your attention, averse to sharing you even with her own offspring.

If your queen has any of these traits or if she is neurotic, bad-tempered, overly aggressive, or extremely nervous, do not breed her.

Last question.

It takes two! Do you have a suitable mate?

Probably not. Perhaps you had assumed that you would take her back to the breeder from whom you bought her. But what if that breeder's only male is your queen's sire? What if the breeder has moved, or gone out of business and sold all stock?

Here you are with a nubile maiden, a bursting desire to mate her, and no male!

The Romeo Quest

"I don't stud out my male to strange queens."

"If your cat has a pedigree going back six generations, I might consider her."

"My fee is $800 and pick of the litter."

"We stud *only* to grand champion females."

These are the kinds of responses one might get when approaching the owner of a stud. For a beginner, finding a male is one of the most frustrating facets of breeding. The average breeder operates a *closed cattery*, which means that only the cattery's females have access to its studs. Occasionally an agreement is made between two breeders who know one another or are working to improve a particular line. But to take in a stranger—out of the question!

Such clannishness may be excused when one considers the value of a well-proven stud, in particular one with an outstanding pedigree. The risks are formidable. An outside queen could bring in ear mites, fleas, fungus, a multitude of devastating diseases. In unfamiliar sur-roundings, she could refuse to eat and become ill from dehydration. She could panic and claw the stud owner or irreparably injure the stud. She might even manage to escape.

If the mating proved successful, the resulting kittens would afford competition on the market or at shows. Their pedigrees would carry the stud's name and cattery, possibly detracting from a reputation that had taken years to build.

But these are stud owners' problems; owners of queens have their own. How does a newcomer to the cat fancy find valid stud service? A truly difficult task, as illustrated by this typical scenario.

A cat show exhibitor informs you of an individual who has open stud service. You make a phone call—after all the negative responses, this one sounds good. The fee is a modest $200, and the stud, according to his owner, a handsome, healthy male.

Before making a commitment, you decide to check out the place. You are appalled. The house reeks of cat urine. The mating quarters turn out to be a dark, dirty bathroom. The stud is a scrawny, cringing tom, coat hanging in patches and eyes running.

An inquiry to the secretary of a cat club takes you to another stud owner. The male looks healthy enough and his papers are in order. But the breeding will take place in a small, unprotected cage in the back yard.

Through an ad in the newspaper a third possibility appears. Alas! The house is floor to ceiling with caged cats. The breeder can't find her champion's papers and said champion resembles the proverbial alley cat.

Dismayed, you are about to give up the whole idea. Then your vet phones to report a new client who owns a whole male. The client operates a registered cattery and under certain conditions would accept an outside queen.

What harm can it do to look? you think, and make an appointment.

The stud is sturdy and friendly with a first-rate pedigree and a current health record. His "bachelor pad" is in the garage, a bright airy room with a large window and tile counters and floor. Everything is immaculate. There's even a smoke alarm above the double-lock door and a night light on the wall.

Grinning inside yourself, you think, Eureka! I've found him!

Maybe you have and maybe you haven't.

A contract for stud service, to coin a phrase, can either make it or break it. The question of fee is the first thing to consider. This can vary dramatically. Usually the charge is based on the male's bloodline, performance, and (possibly) show record—factors that in turn will reflect on the price of his kittens.

A valid stud fee is one that approximates the amount that could be realized from the sale of one kitten. For example, if you were a Siamese breeder and in your area a Siamese kitten without papers went for $150, a stud fee of that amount would be proper. If the stud were a champion, his services would be higher, relative to the value of his offspring. If he were a grand champion, the cost could verge on the astronomical.

In lieu of a monetary fee, the stud owner may opt for *pick of the litter*—a choice of any of the kittens. This does not happen often, as it holds risks for the stud owner. The best kitten may be hidden, or all the kittens may have mysteriously died. Unscrupulous people exist in every field.

As with the amount, the method of payment varies. Some stud owners demand the entire sum up front. Others (and this is more common) ask half the fee when you bring your female and the balance in four weeks, or upon queening.

Whatever the method, be certain the contract contains compensatory provisions in case your queen fails to become pregnant. Such options may include a) one or two return services, b) as many services as necessary, c) refund of half the fee, d) refund of the entire fee. An extra charge for boarding is unusual, but if an entire refund becomes necessary, such a charge is legitimate.

Once in a while a stud owner will tack on conditions relevant to the marketing of the kittens. As breeder-owner, you may be bound to the stipulation that regardless of type, all the kittens be sold with alteration agreements. You may be banned from selling to people with small children, with dogs, or with other cats. The contract may prohibit sales to breeders or, conversely, designate specific breeders or specific areas. Sales to pet stores would be taboo, and justifiably—a conscientious breeder does not deliver her tender young to the haphazard care of a commercial dealer. A stud owner may go so far as to demand immediate notification in the event a kitten is re-sold or given away.

Whatever the terms, the contract should be written in a clear concise manner, dated, and signed by both parties. File your copy; it is your only recourse in case of a disagreement. (See examples of stud contracts in Appendix #3.)

Option: A Romeo of Your Own

Sounds great, doesn't it! But before you dash off to the nearest breeder, consider the pros and cons of investing in a whole male.

On the plus side, you won't have to scour the countryside for the right stud, or transport your queen to him and pay an inordinate service fee. Nor will you be tied to someone else's whims, or face the risk of your queen coming home with ear mites, fungus, or disease. You can breed when you want, where you want. The resulting kittens will be yours to sell to whomever you please and with no picayune conditions.

However (and there are a number of these howevers), the monetary outlay for a stud could make a big dent in your cat-budget. In addition to the purchase price, which could be every bit as high as your queen's, there are housing costs.

Separate quarters for the whole male are essential. A number of stud owners use cages, and while they're not to my liking, cages are acceptable if large enough. In fact, some are quite elaborate, with cooling and heating, piped-in music, beds, ledges, climbing posts, and the like. Alternatives to caging include a walk-in run with a sheltering cat house; a converted shed or a small trailer; the enclosure of a porch or a patio; a room in the garage.

Ownership of a whole male has other negatives besides cost. Your tom will spray, that is almost a certainty—very few virile males do not. Which means that his quarters will need daily cleaning, as well as frequent repairs such as painting. Because of the monetary investment, you may feel obligated to use your male exclusively, which can make it difficult to build a good breeding program. In addition, unless you own a number of queens or accept outside females, your stud could become restless and irritable, and spray more frequently.

Despite such negatives, you may decide to go ahead and buy a whole male. Kitten or adult? Again there are pros and cons. An adult will be proven. You can see his progeny. He will know what to do and how to do it.

On the other hand, toms are extremely territorial, and it may prove difficult for an adult male to adjust. He may even refuse to perform in strange surroundings.

A kitten is the better choice. He will cost less and acclimate quicker. In addition, you'll not have the immediate expense of separate housing.

Like your female, your male should be a registered purebred with good to excellent bloodlines, a four-generation pedigree, and a current health record. He should have been tested for FIP as well as FeLV and preferably been immunized against both. He should be strong in those areas where, according to breed standards, your queen may be weak, such as coat, body conformation, or eye color. A pleasant, outgoing disposition is vital; if the sire is ill-tempered, chances are that his offspring will be the same.

Color depends on your breeding program. You may choose to work with one color alone. For example, if you want to breed *only* Flame Point Himalayans, both sire and dam must be Flame Point (or Cream Point). If variety is desired, a Tortie Point female mated with a Flame Point male would produce a half dozen different colors.

Genetics is a book in itself and it would be impossible to go into its many factors here. In point of fact, a cut and dried genetic rule does not exist. Every breed has its variances, with some colors dominant and some recessive.

A few words of caution before you hand over your money for that male kitten. Examine him thoroughly. If he's going to stud for you, he must have all the fittings. By three months of age, those fittings are usually visible. A male whose testicles have not descended (*cryptorchid*) is infertile. If one testicle is descended (*monorchid*), he *can* breed. It is inadvisable to buy such a male, however, because the condition is hereditary, and it has been known to evolve into cancer.

Shorthair males generally start breeding slightly before their first birthday. Longhairs are slower, sexually maturing at a year to a year and a half. I've known of males who successfully sired at eight months, and others who were almost two before they realized what it was all about. Peak virility seems to be from age two to age eight, although my Shahji was producing large healthy litters at fifteen. Potency appears to be a genetic trait; his sons are the same macho males.

It's easy to tell when a tom is nearing sexual maturity. He grows restless, sometimes irritable. He pursues the females to sniff their rear ends, and tries to mount them. His hormones will force him to relieve himself in ways such as aggression and excessive spraying. Another indication of puberty is cheek enlargement, which leads to the development of those handsome male jowls.

If a male is two years old or more and still shows no interest in breeding, he should be examined by a veterinarian. He may be underweight or have an infection or a hormonal imbalance.

If a male *has* been producing and slacks off, possible causes range from boredom to a hidden illness to overwork. Review his diet; he needs plenty of high protein food. Build him an outside run; he may be getting stir-crazy in the confines of a cage. Bring in an outside queen—perhaps a newcomer to the harem would stimulate the mating urge.

For the most part, males are in the mood most of the time. Like females, however, they have occasional periods of decreased sexual appetite.

Even though you own a stud, keep open your options for outside service. You may need it in case your male matures slowly or becomes ill.

In the meantime, let him get used to his personal quarters by keeping him in them a few hours daily. Permit him to continue the enjoyment of family but gradually lengthen his periods of separation. During his stud room stays, visit him frequently to let him know that he's not being ostracized, that you love him and he is still your boy. Any cat, male or female, who is cuddled, talked to, and petted remains healthy, tractable, and good-natured.

When it becomes necessary for your tom to be permanently isolated, do not feel sorry for him or think you are being cruel. The joyful days of bachelorhood are about to begin.

The Mating Game

By the time a maiden cat reaches her third heat, she is bound to be frustrated. Because she is frustrated, she is bound to take it out on you. She will demand your constant attention—jump on your lap while you're eating, twine around your legs while you're walking, howl at the closed bathroom door. She will roll, groan, squirm, arch her back, and rub against everything in sight. Occasionally you may find drips of urine alongside the litter box instead of in it. The worst will be her midnight *calling*, a discordant caterwauling guaranteed to keep the entire neighborhood awake and to lure to your doorstep every tom within a ten-mile radius.

The quickest way to squelch such exasperating actions is to promptly phone the stud owner with whom you have made previous arrangements.

Ask if it is convenient to bring your queen at this time. If the stud owner agrees, get busy. Clip your queen's nails and check her for fleas. Pack her comb and feeding dish, and anything else you think she might need. Stow her in the cat carrier, and if she is on a special diet, don't forget to bring along her food.

As a rule, it takes a queen twenty-four to thirty-six hours to become acclimated to her strange surroundings, as well as to the strange cat making those strange noises. For a maiden who has never been away from her doting Person, the experience can be terrifying. A practiced stud owner is aware of this and will accept a queen in the early stages of heat to allow her time to adjust.

Cats are induced ovulators, one of the few animals who require the stimulation of mating before releasing eggs for fertilization. Of course, the eggs have to be there in the first place. If the ovaries aren't ripe with eggs, no amount of copulation can make kittens.

Possibly the female knows this, because in the initial phase of heat, she won't let the male near her. Instinct tells her that at the moment her body is preparing itself for the stages to follow. The male watches her warily but keeps his distance. Should he venture close enough to sniff her vulva, a warning growl backs him into a neutral corner.

From this stalemate emerges the *pro-estrus* phase, during which the female begins to invite. She puts on her teasing act—rubs, rolls, stretches, makes little chortling sounds. The male follows her, eagerly sniffing the places she has rubbed. If she urinates, his excitement heightens, stimulated by the scent-signals in her vaginal secretions. He courts her with little chirps and gurgles, all the while circling her, warily watching for a chance to mount. If his impatience propels him to make a move, he is met by a hissing, spitting virago.

She continues to tantalize him with her salacious behavior. She treads, rolls, croons, quivers, clenches and unclenches her paws. Most of the time the male watches her intently, but occasionally he will feign indifference and languidly groom himself or pretend to sleep.

The pro-estrus game can last as long as three days or be as brief as twelve hours. During this time the hapless tom can only wait. Once

in a while the queen might magnanimously allow him to sniff her rump. Just as he thinks she's about to give in, she attacks, and spitting mad, takes off after him. (Which is why a stud's room should offer the refuge of high shelves.)

Eventually the patient tom is rewarded.

The queen enters true estrus, or *standing heat,* when nature signals that the swollen egg sacs in her ovaries are ready to be released. She begins calling, softly at first, then more insistently. She crouches low, with tail switched to the side and rump raised. Her vulva is pointing almost straight upward, an invitation to the waiting tom.

He mounts. He grips the scruff of her neck with his teeth. This ploy freezes her, affording him protection as well as balance for the actual mating. It takes a while to get into the proper position and the queen treads furiously with her rear feet as the male maneuvers. A brief period of pelvic thrusting ensues—then suddenly he inserts his penis.

At this point the queen gives a characteristic cry, whether of rage or pleasure who can say?

Stud: **Chaira's Sultan Saladin of Rajapur,** *BR: Leone Stein, OW/PH: Author*

They break apart, the male making for the safety of a high shelf, the female rolling, spitting, and hissing. After a time she quiets and begins cleaning herself. The male remains in the neutral zone, involving himself in similar activities.

Ten minutes to an hour later the queen again becomes receptive. Mating follows the same general pattern. During the next hours copulation increases as the female becomes more and more demanding.

Eventually the male tires. He watches her from behind half-closed eyes, once in a while mustering enough strength to remount her. In due time his half-hearted efforts cease and he retires to a shelf for a well-earned rest.

The following day finds them still coupling. Some pairs can keep going for a week or longer. A queen *can* ovulate from a single mating, but multiple copulations are more certain.

Actual ovulation takes place twenty-five to thirty hours after an initial contact. The female's hormonal system is set into operation by the stimulation of the penile barbs. These are spines on the penis that, as the male matures and secretes testosterone, grow in size and stiffness. The action of these barbs eventually brings about the release of a hormone that causes the egg-filled sacs in the ovaries to burst open, much like a milkweed plant spilling out its seeds.

Mating initiates not only ovulation but other processes as well, including the production of the progesterone hormone, which prepares the uterus to receive and nurture the fertilized eggs.

After a number of love-sessions, the stud and his queen become quite friendly. They groom each other, snuggle together to sleep, even eat from one another's dish. Mating lessens in frequency and enthusiasm.

During this period, called *metestrus*, the female allows the male to mount her but she becomes angry if he tries to insert his penis.

It may be the tom who decides *enough* and drags himself back to somnolent bachelorhood. Or the queen may revert to her *touch-me-not-anywhere* belligerent self. Whichever, the breeding is finished.

When you are notified to pick up your queen, be prompt. Cleaning and disinfecting a cattery takes time, and the stud owner could have another service coming in.

When your queen arrives home, it's possible she may still be in heat. Be careful that she doesn't get outside. If given the chance, she could actually breed and ovulate again. It's a good idea to bathe her to remove the male odor, which can be a problem if yours is a multi-cat household. Be gentle with the scrubbing; she's bound to be sensitive, particularly around the neck.

Your returning ex-maiden may be brimming over with affection and bubbling with energy. On the other hand, she could be tired and irritable. Cuddle her if she wishes it, but don't feel offended if she prefers solitude to your lap. Offer her food, but don't worry if she refuses it. Go with her mood. After all, she is female, and every female reacts differently after an interlude of lovemaking.

Lady in Waiting

During the first three weeks of pregnancy, you'll see little difference in your queen, except for the cessation of estrus. She will eat, sleep, play, and generally display the same behavior patterns as before. The only variance may be in disposition. The typical pregnant cat becomes very affectionate. Her sexual needs satisfied, she can relax, enjoy her privileged position in the household, and lavish on Her Person the attention that later will be given to her kittens.

Although outwardly your queen may appear unchanged, her inner body is undergoing a complete metamorphosis. You will remember that she became pregnant approximately one day after her first mating when three to six eggs were released from her ovaries to merge with the male's sperm. These minute specks of life called *embryos* take almost two more weeks to become implanted within her uterus. Their nutritional needs are initially met by the yolks from the eggs themselves; then about the twenty-second day, the umbilical cords and the placentas become

sufficiently developed to form the support links between mother and embryos. By this time the bones of the spines are formed and the tiny limbs have taken shape.

Pregnancy is a perfectly natural condition for a cat and seldom do problems arise. A few queens may have *morning sickness*. As with a human mother-to-be, the queasiness and vomiting appear during the first three weeks and abate soon after. The nipples pinken and enlarge near the end of the third or fourth week, particularly if it is a first pregnancy; also, the fuzz around them diminishes.

By the fifth week, the embryos, now called *fetuses*, have developed their internal organs; they are about the size of a pea and can be felt by an experienced hand.

Your queen's appetite may increase at this time, although some females experience a hunger spurt from the very onset of gestation. A well-balanced, high protein diet is essential. Egg yolks and cheese are good sources of protein as well as the usual fowl, fish, and meat. Milk is unnecessary, but give it to her if she craves it and it does not cause diarrhea. If she refuses vegetables, grow grass in a container for her to nibble on. When planning your pregnant queen's diet, diversify with dry, canned, and home-cooked meals. Serve four or five *small* meals daily.

Supplement with extra vitamins and minerals, as advised by your vet. Calcium is particularly important; ask your vet's advice for amount and type.

On rare occasions a pregnant cat will overeat and grow dangerously obese. If your lady-in-waiting turns into a feline glutton, work out a diet with your vet to cut down on starches.

At around five weeks your queen's abdomen will start to round. You may also notice her grooming herself more often, particularly around the nipples and the genital area. This is a good time to have her checked for worms, particularly roundworms — most current worm remedies are safe. Immunizations, however, are rarely given to a pregnant cat. Vets are also cautious about prescribing medication; pain-killing drugs, cortisones, and some of the mycins may cause detrimental side-effects.

It's foolish (as well as futile) to try to restrain the pregnant feline. Running, stretching, and leaping are normal activities, essential to her well-being. Eventually her bulk will slow her down. Weight gain varies from two to four pounds. Most of this gain occurs during the last two weeks, at which time your queen may find herself bewildered and sometimes embarrassed by her unwieldiness.

Because of that unwieldiness, it may become difficult for her to properly clean herself in the genital area. Gently wash with mild soap and warm water those places she is unable to reach. For good hygiene, start clipping the hair around her vulva, anus, and nipples, a little each day. Continue normal grooming, particularly if yours is a longhair.

Be especially alert for fleas — get rid of them *now*. Dips are not recommended, but baths with a flea shampoo are permissible up to the seventh week of pregnancy. Fleas can be a major problem for newborns. I've know cases where tiny kittens have had their lifeblood sucked from them by these voracious insects. (See Tips regarding eliminating fleas on newborns.)

From six weeks on the fetuses will double in size. Their rapid growth may cause pressure on the large intestine, resulting in constipation. Give extra hairball preparation if needed.

During the last two weeks of gestation the kittens become much more active. You can actually see them moving inside the mother's body. This is a warmly emotional time, especially if your queen allows you to feel the new life stirring within her.

Be careful about exposing a pregnant female to other cats; they could be disease-carriers. For similar reasons, and because it would be upsetting, never exhibit a pregnant cat. In fact, don't take her anywhere except to the vet.

Around the seventh week make up your queen's *nest*. This can be anything from a packing carton to a wooden box to the corner of a closet, a cupboard, or a large dresser drawer. I prefer a heavy cardboard carton with a lid—sufficiently roomy for a pregnant female to move about and high enough for her to stand erect.

The first step is to clean and disinfect the carton. Then cut an access hole on the side about three inches up to avoid drafts and to keep the kittens from tumbling out. Or make the opening in the lid, which should be removable to allow access for cleaning and in case the queen needs help during delivery.

Line the nest with newspapers, *heaps* of them. Birth can be bloody—stained newspapers are disposable, stained towels or blankets require laundering. Newspapers give the female in labor a firm foundation and they provide newborns with insulation against cold. Their flat, smooth surface allows kittens to reach mother's nourishing nipples, whereas tiny claws may be caught in the loose weave of a towel or blanket.

Locate the nesting box in a warm, semidark area such as a closet, a spare bathroom, or best of all, the familiarity of your queen's own room. Place near the nest her litter box, water, and food.

Assemble the following items:

A heating pad
A sharp blunt-tipped scissors
Dental floss
Hydrogen peroxide or rubbing alcohol
Vaseline
Several washcloths and small towels
A large trash bag
A small cat carrier
A watch or a clock with a minute hand for timing contractions
    and intervals between births
A pad and a pen to record data for the vet

Your queen will probably find the nest by herself; she will either ignore it or accept it happily. She may decide to rearrange it by shredding the newspapers, pushing them into corners, or nuzzling them into a deeper cavity. Whatever she wants to do, let her! After all, it's *her* nest.

Sita. "So I'm fat—I'm pregnant!" *BR: Steven Stein, OW/PH: Author*

Pregnancy Reversals

Miscarriages can occur in cats as well as in humans, and for similar reasons.

Abortion during *early* pregnancy brings little danger or discomfort; the fetuses are so tiny that they are reabsorbed or easily expelled. A miscarriage in mid or late pregnancy causes problems.

Excessive bleeding is one of them; it rapidly debilitates the dam. An unexpelled fetus rotting inside her may bring on a fiery infection. If your female aborts (or threatens to—bleeding is the typical sign) in mid or late pregnancy, an immediate visit to the vet is indicated.

Some queens have difficulty in conceiving. If a female is repeatedly mated and keeps coming back into heat, an infertile stud may be at fault. In this instance, try another male. Possibly her tubes are blocked; have her thoroughly vet-checked. Such simple procedures as enforced rest, a change of diet, or a series of hormone shots have also been known to help.

Then there is the rare queen who bleeds during estrus. A personal experience with this type of cat had me baffled. Despite repeated matings, she did not conceive. Finally I tried putting her with my stud near the *end* of her estral cycle—it was possible that her flow washed away the sperm.

That did it! She's had two healthy litters and is well on her way to a third.

Once in a while a queen (particularly one who is strictly confined) undergoes a false pregnancy. Her Person will swear that she's not been near a male. Yet here she is making a nest, tenderly carrying to it rolled-up socks and small stuffed animals, cuddling and cleaning them as if they were real kittens. After a time she even swells and her nipples drip with milk.

This peculiar situation is easily corrected. The overly maternal queen is injected with a male hormone. Similar home-medication is prescribed. And thus is ended her sweet delusion.

Again I must stress that false pregnancies, fertility problems, and miscarriages in a cat are unusual, but if the breeding of these paradoxical animals is to become a part of your life, you should be prepared for anything.

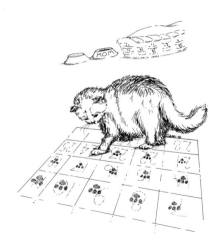

5
BIRTH

Giving Mother Nature a Hand

A queen's due date is figured from the first day she was brought to the stud, with normal gestation lasting sixty-one to sixty-seven days. Which is not to say that pregnancy can't go on longer. I admit to getting nervous when day sixty-nine-minus-kittens arrives. Invariably I call my vet to ask if a shot might be necessary. Invariably he responds with the suggestion that we wait another twenty-four hours.

He's (almost) always right. Mother Nature usually comes through at the proper time and the kittens are born with no problems.

Once in a while even my vet becomes edgy. With day seventy checked off the calendar and the date of mating re-evaluated, X-rays may be indicated (perfectly safe at this stage) to determine the size, position, and number of kittens. If readings prove normal, other explanations are sought.

A typical cause of delay bears the medical name *primary uterine inertia,* which means that no uterine contractions are present, or only ineffective "ripples." In this instance the pregnant queen is injected with calphosan to stimulate the uterus. If the calcium solution proves ineffective, the hormone oxytocin generally brings swift results.

The main reason for medical intervention is to assure the well-being of mother and babies. Kittens that remain in the womb an unduly long time become too large. The queen could be torn during delivery, or worse, be unable to expel them, thus necessitating a costly and traumatic Cesarean section.

Most veterinarians will intervene if circumstances warrant. A few prefer to let nature take its course. I suggest that you confer with your vet beforehand as to his or her policy.

Parturition Signals

About a week before parturition you may notice your queen getting restless. The snug nest you provided may be ignored in favor of the laundry hamper or a closet. She may decide that the carpeting under your bed (if properly shredded) would be even better. *Watch her.* If she has delivery problems, you don't want her stuck some place where you'd be unable to reach her.

A female nearing her time does all kinds of weird things. My Sita wanders about the house, making pathetic little moaning sounds. Sometimes she pulls the towel from her bed and wraps herself in it, or she drags it from room to room. Her behavior bothered me at first, but now I take it in stride, aware that it's an idiosyncrasy of her proximity to queening.

About day sixty-two your lady-in-waiting is likely to demand a larger than normal meal. From then on she will either refuse food or merely nibble. Instinct warns her that undue pressure on her stomach could make her vomit, particularly if she's carrying a large litter.

If her teats have not yet produced milk, they will start to now. Seepage may harden the area around the nipples; to avoid irritation, lay a soft wet cloth on them, then carefully wipe. Toward the end of gestation some breeders lightly coat the teats with mineral, olive, or baby oil.

Other signs will tell you that your queen is drawing near to her time. When she lies down to rest, it will generally be on her side or back. At times she may abruptly stop what she's doing and hurry to the litter box to scratch, squat, and after a few moments clamber out, a perplexed expression on her face. Grooming may become an obsession, particularly around the nipples and the vulva. If yours is a close relationship, she will trail you like a bulky shadow.

On the day preceding parturition, your queen's body temperature will drop from the average 101°/102°F to 99°F. A sticky vaginal discharge will appear, clear in color and often streaked with blood. The clear discharge is normal, but if it has a foul odor or is dark brown or black in color, notify your vet immediately.

When your queen reaches the discharge stage she will likely deliver within a few hours, although some cats excrete mucus for an entire day. A few even dribble for a week or more. For hygienic reasons, and because from now on you'll want to know where she is every minute, put her in her room.

She may or may not get into the nesting box; do not pressure her. Stay with her awhile. Check your supplies again—heating pad? small carrier? scissors, dental floss, Vaseline, towels? Be sure that all windows are closed and the room is warm. During the critical period of parturition, warmth and quiet are essential for a dam's well-being.

Give the vet a call; that individual will appreciate being apprised of the situation. Also have handy an emergency twenty-four-hour phone number. Your queen's usual carrier should be ready in case a fast trip to the vet is indicated.

The last is possible but unlikely. For centuries cats have safely delivered their kittens without human intervention. This does not mean that on your queen's due date you should fritter the day away at the mall or take off on a weekend jaunt. There's a difference with a cat raised in the home as part of the family. Whether or not you actually assist in the birth process, your female will want you near for comfort and support. Queens have even been known to delay parturition until Their Persons could be with them.

On the other hand, at this early stage it is not necessary to closet yourself in her room. Continue your daily routine, pausing at half-hour intervals to peek in.

If you are nervous or feel guilty about leaving your queen alone, then by all means stay. Prepare yourself for what could be a long wait. A thermos of coffee, snacks, perhaps some reading material, and a comfortable chair should see you through.

Labor and Delivery

Labor starts when the involuntary muscles of the abdomen move the first kitten from a horn of the uterus into the pelvic area. At this point your queen will begin panting and you may see the alternately tightening and relaxing of her abdominal muscles. Initial contractions are widely spaced, maybe one every fifteen or twenty minutes. Monitor your queen's progress by jotting down the starting time and the duration of each contraction.

Between contractions the queen cleans herself or licks the sticky discharge on the newspapers. Such actions are instinctive, and it's possible that they help to ease tension. You might also keep occupied. Remove soiled newspapers from the nest and stuff them into a plastic bag. Wrap the heating pad in a hand towel or several layers of newspapers. Set the control at its lowest heat. Plug it in, turn it on, and place it in the small carrier.

As the first kitten moves down the birth canal, the contractions grow stronger and come closer together. Sensing the imminence of birth, your queen may grow increasingly agitated. Her eyes may widen, she may turn around in circles, clean herself, roll onto her side, clean herself again. Each time she senses a contraction coming on, her panting accelerates.

If you notice that your queen is trying to but can't reach the side of the box to push against, offer the flat of your hand. My females like me to put my hand on their abdomens as they push. Yours may not; go with her wishes.

A queen in labor may become panicky and try to climb out of the box, particularly if it is her first birthing experience. Some breeders advocate allowing the female to have her kittens where she wants; they can be returned to the nest later. Others suggest discipline—keep her in the box by restraining her gently but firmly.

If your queen insists on delivering outside the nest, use appropriate measures; you know her temperament best.

It's impossible to state with impunity how long labor will last—like women, queens have different birth rhythms. Suffice it to say that the first kitten to be born usually takes longest and is the most difficult.

At the peak of labor your queen's whiskers will push forward and her face may appear twisted. Her panting will be open-mouthed and extremely rapid. This heavy breathing increases the amount of oxygen in her blood to provide more energy. She may purr or conversely growl and hiss—queening can be a very vocal procedure.

The final in-contraction will go so deep that it bulges her rib cage. When she pushes out, the effort will seem to collapse her chest.

As the first kitten emerges, your queen may groan or cry out. It's unlikely you'll be able to see the newborn because the mother's body will be covering it. You'll know it's arrived because she is no longer straining—her efforts are directed toward removing the membrane around the newborn's head. Once this is accomplished, she will clean herself and her kitten, roughly tongue-massaging the little body to stimulate breathing.

As the kitten's lungs expand to suck in air, it gives its first cry. At that instant the tension that gripped you as you watched your queen strain to give birth will vanish in a surge of joy.

If I sound emotional it's because after all these years of breeding I am still awed by the miracle of birth.

Some kittens are *born* crying. This happens when the fetal membrane is ruptured during delivery. As a rule, the membrane remains intact until the dam uses her teeth to break it, then licks or nibbles it off. If she fails to do this or removes only a part of the membrane, quick action is called for. Emergency situations are discussed later in this segment.

The *placenta*, or *afterbirth*, is expelled either with the kitten or a short time later. If kitten and placenta do not come out simultaneously, the dam again begins straining. Her efforts to rid herself of the afterbirth will appear as if she were trying to deliver another kitten.

For every birth there should be a placenta. Watch for and make a note of each one passed. A placenta looks and feels like a piece of raw liver.

The umbilical cord will still be attaching the newborn to the placenta. Instinct tells the dam to eat the placenta, which is rich in nutrients. After she eats it, she chews on the cord to about an inch from the kitten's belly, where she severs it with her teeth. The stub dries in a day or two and drops off.

Sometimes the process is reversed; the dam parts the cord from the kitten first and then chews down to the placenta.

If there are many kittens, your queen may become filled up with placentas and leave the last one or two. In this instance remove them and flush them down the toilet. The intervals between births can vary from ten or fifteen minutes to an hour. Use this respite to dispose of the soiled newspapers and generally tidy up. The dam will continue cleaning herself and her newborn and perhaps try to rest. The kitten may have a go at nursing—husky ones, especially males, make for the nipples almost immediately.

The second kitten (usually) enters the birth canal from the opposite uterine horn. When labor resumes, *remove the first kitten* and place it on the heating pad inside the carrier—that way there'll be no chance that the mother will accidently step or roll on it. The kitten is unable to nurse anyway while its mother is in labor.

After the second kitten has been born and licked clean, put the first one back into the nest. Help each baby find a nipple. Follow this procedure throughout the queening.

The next kittens are born in a similar manner but more easily, because the passage has been widened and moistened by those preceding them. By the fourth or fifth kitten, your queen may start to tire. If she will permit, help her by drying any wet kittens with a warmed towel, the lastborn first.

Giving birth to four or five kittens can take the better part of a day. Or it can occur as rapidly as a birth every ten or fifteen minutes. With a first-time mother, parturition usually goes slowly.

A word of warning. If your queen has *strong, regular* contractions lasting longer than an hour and no births result, call your vet. An overlarge kitten (or a dead one) could be blocking the canal.

Before leaving your queen, make certain that she is relaxed and each kitten is nursing. Close the door and leave the new family alone for an uninterrupted hour or two.

When you return, bring a dish of dry food and a bowl of fresh water. Set the water next to the nest, the food inside it. The first day or two most dams won't leave their babies even to eat. Don't be concerned if the mother ignores the food; if she devoured all the placentas, she won't want it. Have her litter box nearby, since she *will* want that. A mother cat is as fussy as a Dutch hausfrau when it comes to an immaculate environment for her young.

Important. Within a day after birth or even sooner, take mother and babies to be vet-checked. It is simpler and safer to transport them in separate carriers; vets (and owners) have been known to be clawed when trying to remove kittens from an overly protective mother. A shoebox will do for the kittens; lay a small, warmed towel on the bottom, and perforate the cover for ventilation.

The vet may give your dam an oxytocin injection to start minor contractions; this expels any blood clots or bits of placenta and also brings down more milk. The kittens will be examined, their cords checked, they may be weighed, and very definitely admired.

Birth Complications

Problems in queening are unusual, but sometimes they happen. Before going into emergency measures, I offer the following advice:

1. *Do not interfere unless it is absolutely necessary.*
2. *Know what you're doing and keep calm.*
3. *If possible, consult your vet first.*

Appropriate measures for the overdue queen have already been mentioned. Unfortunately, one can do little when the mother delivers too soon. If the kittens are only a day or two premature, immediate medical care may help one or two of the strongest ones to survive. For births that occur before sixty days of gestation, chances of making it are practically nil.

Normally a kitten is born head first, with the front legs stretched out alongside the head and the belly facing down. The opposite, with back legs emerging first (commonly but erroneously called *breech*) is also normal, although often more difficult. A true breech occurs when only the rump and the tail protrude and the rest of the kitten is still inside the mother.

Other complex birth positions include: only one leg protruding, the kitten emerging on its back instead of its belly, a birth in which the body is shaped like an L, the head twisted or turned backward.

These are rare instances, and chances are slim that you'll need to cope with them. Here are a few suggestions, though, just in case.

With a *stuck* kitten, give the dam about ten minutes to expel the baby on her own. If she is unable to, try these measures.

Using a washcloth or a small hand towel, grip as much of the kitten's body as you can. Try to adjust its position by moving it back into the mother's vagina and turning it slightly. Then pull *gently* in rhythm with the mother's pushes and pauses. *Do not jerk or pull straight out, pull in a circular fashion, first toward and then away from the mother's abdomen.* The kitten's body must be eased from the vaginal opening the way a cork is eased from a bottle.

Another cause of a kitten being stuck is *dryness of the vaginal tract;* the dam may have lost too much fluid due to prolonged labor. Load a cotton swab with mineral oil, olive oil, or Vaseline; insert and gently run it halfway around the inside of the birth canal. Load it again and repeat on the other half. On the next contraction, help the dam with slight tugs as previously instructed.

After its long struggle to be born, the kitten may appear lifeless. Do not wait for the dam to act. *Immediately* peel the membrane from the head, using your fingers, a washcloth, or a dry paper towel. Wipe the kitten's nose, mouth, and inside the mouth, and rub down its body.

At this point the kitten should gasp, sputter, and begin breathing. If it does not, it is because the lungs and/or mouth are still filled with fluid. To expel the fluid, wrap the kitten in a towel, head exposed, turn it upside down, and swing it in a wide arc. Do this three or four times, *being very careful to support the head and the neck.*

If that doesn't work, try these alternative measures:

1. Massage the kitten from head to toe with a heated towel. Don't be overly gentle—when the dam licks her newborn, she does so with vigor.
2. Wrap the kitten in a heated towel. Bring its face close to yours and blow into it five *little* puffs of air. Pause; then repeat. Continue until the kitten cries and starts breathing. Patience and persistence are required for the "puff" method, but generally it works. I've used it on a number of occasions and only twice was I forced to the more extreme measure that follows.
3. Immerse the kitten in a basin of very warm water, up to its neck. Keep it there a minute or two. Remove and towel vigorously. Follow up with the shakedown swing to expel any fluid. If unsuccessful the first time, try it again. I had to dip one little guy four times before he started sputtering.

I might add that none of the kittens revived by these methods suffered any ill effects, and their mothers accepted them without reservation.

As a rule, newborns will breathe on their own within sixty to ninety seconds after birth. If a kitten feels cold and limp and isn't breathing, don't just shrug and give up. *Act!* An immediate response, coupled with persistence, can save a tiny life.

Which is not to imply that you will never suffer a kitten loss. Every breeder I know has had to go through that sorrow at one time or another. It's a part of breeding that one has to accept, painful though it may be.

Occasionally problems arise concerning the afterbirth. A second kitten may be emerging from the birth canal while the first is still attached to its placenta. Or the placenta may not yet be expelled.

This is a situation that always distresses me. I see this tiny kitten dangling from its cord, one end of which is attached to its belly and the other end to the placenta, which is still inside the mother's vagina. Meanwhile, the mother is resting or placidly cleaning herself or, distressing sight! thrashing about, trying to dislodge another kitten. What do I do—stand by and watch the newborn get stepped on or whacked against the side of the box? Or take the initiative and cut the cord?

Some breeders say leave it alone. They insist that the kitten cannot be harmed, that it is still partly protected by the fetal membranes and in due time the cord will break by itself. The problem with this is that we do not know if the placenta is still attached to the uterus to provide the kitten with blood and oxygen. In addition, the cord could be crimped by a second kitten, thus strangling the first.

Another (and better) suggestion is to pick up the kitten and try to move it with the mother—that way it's unlikely to get a hernia because of being dragged by the cord.

A third alternative is to either pinch off the cord with the fingers or snip it with a blunt-tipped sterilized scissors.

I take action *if:*

1. The dam is so agitated that she may harm the kitten.
2. The dam is too exhausted or too confused to do it herself.
3. The births are so rapid that the kittens are piled one on top of the other.

On the other hand, moving *too* fast can cause mishaps. I felt terrible the time my scissors slipped and clipped off the tip of a newborn's tail. Frankly, I panicked—Sita was wildly swinging the first kitten around by its cord while trying to expel the second (which later turned out to be a five-ounce male). The fact that I was going entirely by feel was small consolation. I should have held the first kitten and waited until the second was expelled or until the position of the dam allowed me to see better.

A prolonged labor or an unusually large litter may make the mother too tired to bite off the final umbilical cord, or a frightened, inexperienced dam may ignore the entire process. In such cases, intervention is called for.

Before cutting the cord, give the kitten an extra boost by squeezing the placenta, thus forcing vivifying blood into its body. Using a sharp, sterilized, blunt-tipped scissors, snip the cord about an inch and a half from the kitten's body. If there is bleeding, tie off the cord near its base, using sterilized thread or dental floss, and apply to the tip a dab of boric acid powder.

Never pull on the umbilical cord in an attempt to dislodge a placenta inside the dam; cut it instead.

Never allow a newborn to dangle or be yanked around by the cord; hold the kitten in your hand.

Do not try to manage these procedures alone; if possible, have someone with you to control the dam.

In the majority of births, kittens and placentas are expelled with no problems, a fact that should be reassuring to the novice breeder.

Occasionally a queen gives no sign that she's about to go into labor. Her unsuspecting Person awakes one morning to discover her in the closet, happily snuggling a quartet of newborns. This is the fortunate outcome. It's a fifty-fifty chance that Her Person could just as well arrive home to find a bleeding, bewildered dam, and cold, limp kittens scattered about the house.

If the latter should happen, there is still a chance to recoup.

Gather up the kittens and wrap them in anything at hand. Then toss some towels into a clothes dryer set on high. Search the house for any newborns you may have missed. When the towels are toasty warm, transfer the kittens. Several of the babies may still have life in them; attempt the resuscitation methods previously described.

If a kitten does not respond after fifteen minutes, give it up and move on to another. Keep those you have saved on a heating pad while you notify your vet.

One of the post-partum problems the dam may incur is *bleeding.* A slight amount of blood is normal for about a week after queening. It may be just an occasional drip or occur only when the queen is straining to relieve herself. This type of bleeding usually stops naturally.

Emergency care is indicated if there is

1. constant excessive bleeding
2. a sudden rush of blood (possibly a hemorrhage)
3. a high fever
4. pain or agitation in the dam

Another potential complication is a retained placenta or fetus—either can spell *big trouble.* The dam becomes lethargic and discharges a heavy brown substance. Her abdomen is painful, and she refuses to eat or to nurse her kittens. Her temperature rises alarmingly. Infection usually follows, with sometimes fatal results.

This distressing situation is completely unnecessary; it can be avoided by having the dam vet-checked soon after queening.

Other post-partum complications include: prolapse of the uterus, blood blisters in the vulva, mastitis, inflamation of the uterus; and toxic shock, usually fatal. Such problems are infrequent. Be assured that if caught early enough, modern medicine will take care of them.

The Imperfect Kitten

One facet of breeding that most cat-raisers dislike talking about is the stillborn kitten or the deformed one.

Regretfully, stillborns are quite common with cats, particularly with maiden queens. The tightness of the virgin birth canal may be one cause of a kitten being born dead. Or it could be attributed to the confusion and occasional panic of an inexperienced female.

Nature has her quirks, too. An undeveloped fetus can be carried full term and delivered normally but dead. Or a fully developed but weak or overlarge kitten may die while still in the uterus or the birth canal.

As with human babies, defects can occur for no apparent reason (except inbreeding too often). Kinked tails and cleft palates are not uncommon. Nor are extra toes unusual; cats with these are called *polydactyls.*

Generally speaking, there's no cause for worry if the examination of a newborn reveals a slight heart murmur or a small umbilical hernia. The heart usually corrects itself and the hernia can be repaired by surgery. Your vet will know whether or not it is a serious problem.

The Newborns

The number of kittens in a litter is relative to breed, size, nutrition, and genetics. Four appears to be average. Shorthairs, like the Siamese, produce large litters and deliver with ease, primarily because of body structure. Persians and Himalayans tend to have a harder labor; large heads, broad shoulders, and stocky bodies don't slip out as smoothly as long, slender ones.

A newborn can weigh as much as five ounces or as little as one; the average is three. Genetics, nutrition, and breed are again the determining factors. A small litter or an overlong gestation will produce larger kittens.

The typical dam has eight teats, so presumably she could nurse that many kittens. However, while the middle and back breasts are heavy with milk, usually those in the front have little. Seven or eight sucklings would not only rapidly lessen the milk supply, they would drain the mother's health. If the litter numbers a half dozen or more, or if several are runts, supplemental feedings may become necessary. (More on this later.)

First milk is a thin liquid called *colostrum*. Rich in protein and minerals, colostrum's primary importance lies in its antibodies. If something happens to keep the kittens from nursing during the short period of colostrum production, they become more vulnerable to disease and therefore should be immunized as young as four or five weeks.

The most critical period of a kitten's life is its first thirty-six hours. *Warmth* is every bit as important as food. A newborn's fur gives little protection because it's so sparse; consequently, body heat is lost rapidly. Which is why tiny kittens so often die from chilling.

During that pivotal first week I keep a heating pad inside the nest or a heat lamp above it. Newborns have undeveloped thermostats; therefore, careful supervision is required to avoid overheating.

Care and Feeding of Newborns

Some dams produce inferior milk, others have insufficient production, and there is the unusual dam who refuses to nurse her babies. In these instances someone else has to take over maternal duties.

Intervention is also necessary if the queen develops any kind of infection, especially mammary or uterine.

When for whatever reason the queen is unable to suckle her newborns, the suggestion always seems to be *find them a surrogate mother*. I've never been fortunate enough to locate a nursing dam who would accept the tiny strangers. Perhaps the solution would be to program matings, allowing two females to queen about the same time.

Meanwhile, circumstances have occasionally forced me to become a surrogate mother to one or more furry babies. If you find yourself cast in a similar role, be prepared to give up your sleep. During their first week of life, newborns need to be fed every two to four hours.

You can make your own kitten formula by mixing a can of evaporated milk, an equal amount of boiled water, an egg yolk, and a tablespoon of Karo syrup, dark or light. A better alternative is to have on hand one of the commercial kitten formulas, the best-known being Borden's KMR. A mother's milk replacement can be expensive, but it is well worth the cost because of its carefully balanced blend of a kitten's essential needs. The powdered form of KMR is more economical than the liquid but not as convenient (see Tips for advice on mixing).

Most pet stores carry the kitten formulas as well as small nursing bottles and nipples. I find a plastic dropper is easier to use the first week of nursing.

If you need to supplement, sterilize everything—bottles, nipples, measuring cup, spoons, storage container, funnel, mixing tools. Use the following or a similar feeding procedure:

Warm the replacement milk to room temperature (test on your wrist). If necessary, enlarge the nipple hole with a sterilized needle. Remove one kitten from the nest. Seat yourself in a comfortable chair and cover your lap with a towel. The towel will protect your clothing, keep the kitten warm, and give it something to cling to. The warmed milk, along with a few tissues, should be within easy reach.

Cradle the newborn *on its stomach* in the palm of one hand. With your index finger carefully open the kitten's mouth. Holding the bottle in the other hand, place the nipple against the side of the mouth and squeeze out a drop of milk.

The kitten's initial reaction will be to drool the milk. Tissue-wipe its chin. Now squeeze out several more drops—the baby has had its first taste.

Insert the nipple, resting it against the lower jaw at a 45-degree angle. Close the kitten's mouth. Here's where endurance and patience come in. The kitten will squirm and drool. The milk will flow slowly. Sometimes one may sit holding the bottle for fifteen minutes before discovering the nipple is clogged!

Encourage the newborn to suck by slightly pulling the bottle or by moving the nipple around in its mouth. Don't let the kitten nurse too fast or it will draw in air—a distended abdomen indicates gassiness.

If holding the kitten in your hand while feeding it feels awkward, sit at a table and place the kitten, stomach down, on the table's toweled surface.

After nursing, burp the feline baby by putting its head on your shoulder or by laying it on its stomach in your lap and gently rubbing its back.

Often a kitten will stop nursing because of exhaustion. Make certain it is full before giving it to the dam to clean and to stimulate elimination.

If the newborn is orphaned, you must take over such maternal duties. Encourage elimination by gently rubbing the anal area with a warm, moist cotton ball. Note the residue on the cotton; normal feces are creamy-yellow and fairly soft, about the consistency of toothpaste. *The first two weeks of life newborns cannot eliminate on their own; it is vital that you conclude each feeding with anal stimulation.*

If a kitten becomes constipated, add to the formula a tiny amount of honey or Karo syrup. Or use a dibble of Laxatone or another hairball preparation.

If diarrhea is a problem, a few drops of Kaopectate will usually relieve it. In addition, dilute the milk by half or substitute water for *one* feeding. An over-rich formula can make the bowels loose.

During the first week feed newborns in amounts of 1 to 1½ teaspoonfuls every three or four hours around the clock. The second week eliminate late-night feedings, four or five during the day should suffice. A good rule to follow is to give just enough formula to slightly round the belly.

Weigh the kittens daily on a postal scale for the first week; every other day after that. Don't be concerned if there is no immediate gain; it's quite acceptable if weight stays even the first few days. After that, weight gain should average ¼ to ½ ounce daily. Birth weight should be almost doubled by the end of the first week.

Another type of supplemental feeding is the tube method. Seasoned breeders sometimes use this technique for weak or sick kittens. For the novice, this method may be hard to manage. It requires explicit instructions from a veterinarian, who will calculate the amounts to feed as well as supply the proper size and length of tube.

Orphan kittens need daily grooming. Even if the eyes are still closed, dab them lightly with a cotton ball moistened in a mild boric acid solution. To clean the coat and to stimulate circulation, wipe down the entire body with a warm, damp washcloth; then towel dry. If a kitten is excessively soiled, sponge with a dilution of baby shampoo, rinse, and dry. Providing the room is warm, it won't hurt to get the kitten wet; remember, it was born that way.

Without a mother to snuggle them, the greatest danger to orphan kittens is *chilling*. Keep them on a heating pad, or use an overhead infrared lamp. Place or hang a thermometer in the nest. For the first five days, keep the temperature at 90°F. Keep it at 85° for the next week, then gradually decrease it to around 75°. If a kitten gets too warm, it will usually inform you by panting or by moving off the heating pad.

One more suggestion for orphaned or ignored newborns. Give them individual nests. I learned this the hard way when one of my kittens came down with a genital infection. My vet told me that because of their innate need to suck, orphan kittens frequently "nurse" on their littermates' tails, ears, or genitalia. So keep them apart the first few weeks; one possibility is to divide shoeboxes into compartments.

The Handling of Newborns

So many times I've been asked, *When can I start handling the kittens?* To which I invariably respond, *Immediately!* From the moment of birth, touch and caress those soft little bundles of fur. This is the ideal way to socialize them, to accustom them to being with humans. Don't be afraid of harming them, they're not eggshells to break at a touch. Just be careful to pick them up properly and hold them securely.

Another premise is that removing a small kitten from the nest is psychologically harmful to both mother and baby. Don't believe it — *handling forms a bond.* It is not to be feared but rather, encouraged. Merely remember not to interrupt the kittens' sleeping or nursing.

So hold those new babies, cuddle them, talk to them. Love emanates from the gentle stroking of your fingers, the softness of your voice. Those wee snippets of life can't help but sense that love and respond in kind.

Katzenburg's Natasha & Sasha, Russian Blue female kittens—BR: *Ingeborg Urcia,* OW/PH: *Paul Aoki*

6
THE KITTENS

The First Two Weeks

"Helpless as a newborn kitten."

We're all familiar with this aphorism, and in essence it's true. Kittens are born deaf, blind, and toothless. They're unable to move their bowels unassisted, and their legs are so weak that they have to slither on their stomachs to reach their mother's teats. Minutes after birth a fawn will falter to its feet, ready to flee if danger threatens. A newly hatched rattlesnake can protect itself with poisonous fangs. Although fish are deserted as soon as spawned, nature has prepared them to fend for themselves. None of these survival skills were designed for feline babies—they are completely dependent on their mother for food, warmth, and security.

On the other hand, kittens do not come into this world totally weaponless. They have claws—long, sharp, and destructive. They have startlingly loud voices, as anyone who has heard a kitten's scream of fright will attest. They have spunk—even before its eyes open, a startled newborn will hiss at an intruder.

Of the nine feline senses, three are fully developed at birth. Kittens can *feel* the warmth of their mother's body. They can *smell* her milk. They can *taste* its distinctive flavor. These three senses act like beacons to give them yet a fourth—the sense of *direction*.

Sense of direction leads to food, and food is the driving force of a newborn's existence.

At birth the average kitten is little more than three inches long, but it possesses the tenacity of a mongoose. It is an education in perseverance to watch a kitten barely out of the womb strive to reach the nourishment of its mother's breasts. The back legs push as the front legs flail while the head bobbles from side to side, blindly seeking the odors of mother and milk. Once the warmth of the dam's body is felt, the kitten works its way along the nipples, pushing and nuzzling until it finds the teat it will mark for its own. For the first few weeks the kitten will fight for that teat, kicking, clawing, and squealing its outrage if a littermate tries to usurp it.

Initially the milk flows freely; all that is needed is to mouth the nipple and swallow. In a day or so the stream slows. Instinct tells the kitten to *knead* the breast in order to pump milk into the nipple. This pushing with one paw and then the other evolves into a rhythmic movement accompanied by purring. The kneading-purring behavior continues into maturity as an expression of deep contentment.

A nursing dam's milk is highly nutritious. It has considerably less sugar than human milk, ten times as much protein, and 70 percent more fat. To maintain this richness, serve your queen small portions of *vitamin-supplemented, high protein food* four to five times a day. Keep her water fresh, her grooming light, and her nest clean and warm. After a week, remove most of the newspapers from the box and line it with a soft blanket or towel. Launder the lining every other day.

The kittens' eyes should start to crack at the corners at about one week. Twice a day thereafter gently wipe the eye area with a cotton ball moistened in a mild boric acid solution. If despite your attention the lids become gummy and stick together, your vet can prescribe an ointment.

By two weeks at the latest the eyes should be fully open. Trim the front claws at this time to prevent injury to littermates. *Keep the room semidark* — newly opened eyes are highly sensitive to light. Initial eye color is blue or blue-grey; this gradually changes to a color typical of the breed.

A kitten's first look at the world is blurred because it cannot focus, but the fuzziness rapidly clears. Feline vision is remarkably keen. Cats see best in dim light, however, which is why they prefer to hunt at dusk. Although they look forward as we do, they can detect the slightest of movements from their eye corners. Their judgment of distance is comparable to ours, but their color conception is inferior. Still, unlike dogs, they *can* distinguish one color from another.

At birth a kitten's ears are flat against its head. The ears begin to open about the same time as the eyes. Sound is taken in from the outer corners, and partly because cats are able to move their ears at will, feline hearing is much more acute than human hearing.

From the very beginning, and particularly when their mother is not around, kittens depend on each other for warmth and security. When they're not nursing, they lie in a mound, one on top of the other. As their legs are not strong enough for climbing, they make the mound by burrowing.

Once the mound is formed, it stays intact for a while. Then the kitten on top starts to squirm. One can almost hear it complaining *I'm cold! Gotta find me a warmer spot.* The kitten slides down from the top of the mound to dig into the toasty bottom, thus rousing its sleeping littermates. After squeaky protests, the babies drift off, only to have another chilled kitten disrupt their slumber.

Not that tiny felines sleep peacefully. They jerk, kick, squirm, sigh, and make funny little sucking noises. Eyelids quiver and faces grimace, and one can't help but wonder what they are dreaming of.

If you're the typical novice, you've likely been wondering about other things, and to that end (no pun intended!) been lifting tails, trying to differentiate sexes. You'll remember that the anus is the top opening; below it a female will have a slit that, when combined with the anus, looks like the letter "i." The male's opening is rounder and farther down from the anus; also, a male tends to have broader shoulders and a larger head.

Sexes determined, and the critical first two weeks weathered, apply for a *litter application form* from the association with which your queen is registered. Preferably that will be CFA, the only registry recognized by all others including foreign. If not CFA, it would be to your advantage to register with them later.

Developmental Milestones

Kittens become roamers around three weeks of age. Within the confines of the nest they crawl about in aimless circles. When a couple

Female   &   Male

of wanderers meet and want to pass, one burrows under the other and then each continues on its purposeless way. Sometimes a wee rover will drop off to sleep in a far corner of the box. Check the nest often; removed from the warmth of mother and littermates, a kitten could quickly chill.

About this time the dam herself may decide to do some moving, a practice that likely goes back to a distant past when it was dangerous to remain too long in one place. Using her teeth, she picks up a kitten by its scruff and very carefully carries it to a new nest. She goes back and forth a number of times to make sure no kittens are left behind. If the neck fur is too short for the mother to get a good grip, she may mouth the kitten's head and carry it that way. I mention this because the first time I saw my queen slink by with a tiny body dangling from her mouth I panicked, thinking she was eating her kittens!

Dams have been known to move their litters at an earlier age but seldom later, as the babies grow too heavy to be toted around. When my queens try to move their litters, I insist on putting them back in their box. Eventually the dam accepts my decision.

Three weeks finds the kittens starting to *look* like kittens. At birth, and for a time after, their skinny bodies, long heads, and sparse hair makes them resemble baby mice more than baby felines. With my Himmies, at three weeks I can see heads broadening, bodies rounding, and points coming in. Fuzz has been replaced by fluffy fur and tails

look like tails instead of ropes. With their plump paws and flower faces they are becoming precious miniatures of their mother.

Longhair or shorthair, the changes taking place can't help but delight the breeder. You'll notice that the kittens are awake for longer periods. When asleep, instead of mounding, they sprawl with chins or legs resting on one another. They make vague attempts at play, but eye and body are not well enough coordinated and their bats at the air look like they're shadowboxing. Awake or asleep, they artlessly arrange themselves in eyecatching poses—start taking those snapshots for your album and for future buyers.

Between three and four weeks the kittens grow aware of things other than food, warmth, and mother. One might liken them to toddlers on the brink of entering nursery school. They sense that they're ready to move on but are timid about taking that first step. Put a toy mouse in the nest and they will back away from it or raise their hackles and hiss. Eventually the boldest kitten may paw the alien object—not to play with it but to warily inspect it. A similar uncertainty marks their feelings about their environment. Remove a kitten from the nest and it cries; put it back and it scratches to get out.

Rajapur Seal Point Kitten. "Where's my mommy!" – OW/PH: *Author.*

It's time to give your feline babies a little encouragement.

During the day occasionally take them from the nest and let them creep around on a carpet or blanket. With the strengthening of their legs, you'll soon see them walking without bellies dragging. Senses are being stimulated as small noses investigate the toe of your shoe or a fascinating spot on the blanket. A rough little tongue may lick the salt from your hand or you may catch a wandering kitten lifting its paw in surprise as it touches the cold hardness of a tiled floor. An entire new world is opening for these wee explorers.

If you have frequently handled the kittens, as suggested, your queen should not be unduly upset when she sees them out of the nest. A dam who is nervous by nature, however, may need to be isolated. I've found that in due time the most protective of mothers will relax, even to stretching out on the blanket to nurse her babies.

If feasible, share part of your evening with the kittens. Bring them in a basket into the living room. Give each an individual love-time, snuggled in your lap while you sit in an easy chair. Have the television on to accustom them to unfamiliar voices and sounds. At this age they are particularly sensitive to loud noises, so keep the sound low.

From four weeks on, personalities start to unfold; as children do in a human family, each kitten is developing into an individual. One

may already be fussy about its appearance, grooming at every opportunity. Another may be a lover, constantly wanting to be held. It seems
there's always a klutz that bumps into things and trips over its own
feet. And then there's the "all boy" type, living up to his name by swiping
nipples and picking fights.

The small bodies suddenly epitomize energy in motion. The kittens
climb, run, pounce, jump, wrestle, arch their backs, and threaten with
their cunning sideways prance. Play becomes rowdy, often heated if
a kitten decides to try out its milk teeth on a handy tail. They nurse
greedily, squabbling among themselves as to which nipple belongs to
whom. Weight averages four times that of birth.

Vocabulary has expanded—they chortle, growl, gurgle, and chirp.
Their curiosity is boundless; if left free to explore, they won't miss a
crack or a corner. That curiosity also applies to tasting everything within
reach. Which means that your housekeeping has to be flawless, at least
until the small epicures learn the difference between cat food and
dustballs.

Gradually allow the energetic youngsters short periods of house
exploration, but make certain that you are free to keep an eye on them.
Have a spray bottle handy to warn would-be drapery and furniture
climbers, and keep bedroom doors closed to foil under-bed hiders.

Relative to your circumstances, introduce the small felines to the
outside world. On a warm afternoon, carry a kitten into the back yard
or the garden. Hold it snugly; it's bound to be awed, even frightened

by the openness. Titillate its senses by letting it sniff a conifer or a flower. Let it watch a butterfly or a bird in flight. Encounters like these are a treat as well as an aid to development.

I can hear some of you saying, *Why take a kitten outside if it is to be an inside cat?*

It's been my experience that kittens confined within four walls become terrified when exposed to the outdoors. Those introduced to the wider world adapt readily to trips to the vet, the groomer, a show, an outside cat run, and eventually a new home.

By five weeks the kittens have learned to differentiate between humans, often shrinking from strange voices or squirming when being held by someone with an unfamiliar odor. They know Their Person immediately; the moment you enter their room, they scamper toward you, making little chortling sounds. They twine around your legs or try to climb them; if you sit on the floor, they clamber over you, nibble your fingers, tug at your clothing. They love having you at their level and they voice their pleasure in throaty rumbles.

Part of their joy at having you with them may be because Mom is not around as much. When she is with them, she is not as attentive as in the past. She seems reluctant to nurse—to keep a kitten from suckling she will hold it down with her paws and lick it so vigorously that when released, it is only too glad to run off. She may even cuff the more obstreperous youngster, or lay her ears back and give a warning hiss as the hungry horde bounces toward her.

It is apparent that your queen is trying to tell you something. So are the kittens—although they continue to nurse, you may catch them sniffing around their mother's food. The day you find the dam's feeding dish overturned and evidence of "who dunnit" stuck on small paws and clinging to tiny whiskers, you'll know that weaning time has arrived.

Every breeder has a favorite weaning formula. Let me give you mine.

Spoon a small amount of an instant baby cereal, such as Gerber's Baby Oatmeal, into a mixing bowl. Slowly stir in KMR liquid formula until the oatmeal is the consistency of thick soup. If KMR is unavailable, diluted evaporated milk or filtered water may be used.

The mixture should be smooth. It should be warm, but not hot. It should be served in a shallow dish with raised edges to eliminate spilling.

It's easier on your back if you begin by placing the dish of cereal on a newspapered counter or table. It's easier on your nerves if you remove mother cat from the room. It's easier on your clothing if you cover it with an overlarge apron. And it's easier all around if necessities like paper towels, damp washcloths, and tiny bibs are within reach.

Stand a kitten on the counter and bib it. Hold it firmly with one hand as you dip the (scrubbed) forefinger of the other into the cereal and dab it on the kitten's tongue. The kitten may bite. It may cry. It may squirm to get free. Ignore any negative response and keep dabbing. Try putting a dollop of cereal on its nose—it may lick it off.

Make brief this initial solid-food feeding. After wiping the oatmeal-smeared face, put down the first kitten and start on the next.

Offer the cereal two or three times a day. One kitten may accept the new food eagerly, another half-heartedly, while a third totally rejects it. *Persist and insist.* A morning will come when your furry babies greet you with noisy demands for their breakfast—I guarantee it!

Once the kittens become receptive, let them go it on their own. Use individual dishes placed on a newspapered floor. Or try a "community dish," such as a small pie tin; often a kitten will be drawn to food when it sees another eating. Be sure to remove the dam when you feed her kittens or she may take a notion to join them.

Start adding to the cereal ingredients such as cooked mashed egg yolk, meat baby food, or canned chicken cat food. Taper off the cereal and eventually eliminate it. Then try a dry kitten food such as Iams, water-softened to a mushy consistency. Kittens of this age should *not* be given fish, liver, kidney, or meat by-products; serve only beef, chicken, or lamb.

Under six weeks of age, feed four or five times a day in individual amounts of one to two teaspoonfuls. After eight weeks ease back to three feedings daily, with a bedtime snack.

Fast-growing kittens need a complete vitamin and mineral supplement. Pills, unless mashed, are difficult for small throats to swallow. Use either liquid or powder supplements and consult your vet as to brand. Growing kittens also need more fat; for four kittens, add one teaspoon of melted butter to their bowl of food.

For a time-saving convenience, mix up a week's food supply and spoon single servings into ice cube trays to freeze. The feedings easily pop out to thaw or to be warmed in the microwave.

Kittens will suckle as long as their dam lets them. If your queen is the overly maternal type who, nips or no nips, adores being sucked on, keep her from her babies during the day but allow her to nurse them at night. This method will dry her up gradually. If her nipples cake or her breasts harden, cut back on her food. Alleviate breast discomfort by applying warm wet packs on the involved area.

Litter box training seldom presents problems. Once the kittens start eating solid food, the mother refuses to clean them, so the youngsters look elsewhere. Most people believe that the dam teaches her kittens proper elimination habits. Imitation plays a part, but as a rule the kittens teach themselves, drawn by odor and instinct.

They can use your help, though. Make sure the box is low enough for short legs to manage. Keep it clean. Place it in a convenient spot and leave it there. A kitten tends to eliminate soon after eating, so to establish a routine, place it in the box when it finishes a meal.

There always seems to be one kitten who is either stubborn or slow. After it eats, place it in the box. Massage gently under its tail with a damp cotton ball to stimulate elimination.

Manis of Sayang, Singapura Sepia Agouti female with four kittens
—*BR/OW: Douglas Pollock & Wilson Vegas, PH: Douglas Pollock*

Kittens, like children, can ignore nature's call when they are having fun. If accidents happen, do not spank the small malefactor or rub its nose in the excrement. Place the kitten in the box. Wait to see if more is coming. Then clean up.

A kitten recently introduced to solid food may have an occasional runny movement. Always check small bottoms after box use. If soiled, sponge off with a soft damp cloth or wash in a basin of warm water.

If yours is a multi-cat household, carefully supervise kitten contacts with the other felines. Although a strong maternal instinct governs the typical female, jealousy may develop. Play may become too rough or kittens grow overly aggressive, their persistent attacks testing the patience of their elders. An extremely protective dam may attack another cat if it gets too near her babies.

Be extra cautious if a male is around; some toms, particularly feral or barn cats, have been known to kill their offspring. Most males, though, will sniff a kitten and then stalk away. Occasionally one sees a stud like my Saladin who so dotes on his babies that he allows them to suck on him!

Six weeks after parturition, or even earlier, a queen is apt to go back into season. Once in a while it's a false estrus, but more often it's the real thing. Use the same precautions as before; a female's first sampling of romance is bound to whet her appetite for more.

Providing she had no problems, your queen may be bred again in six to eight months. Have her vet-checked first, and the necessary boosters given.

Rajapur's Mimi & Minu-ette, Himalayan Flame Point female kittens, BR: *Elaine Gilbertson,* OW: *Paulette Little,* PH: *Ron Burgis*

7
THE KITTEN MARKET:
DOLLARS AND SENSE

The Preliminaries

Like any other venture, the marketing of kittens requires preparation. Within three or four weeks of your request you should receive the litter application form from your queen's registry. Enter the necessary information and sign it. The stud owner must also sign to authenticate the sire. Return the application along with a check or money order to cover the fee noted on the reverse side.

It takes two to four weeks for the registry to respond with a *certificate of litter registration* showing that the kittens are registered *as a group.* File the certificate, which has a referral number in case correspondence is necessary. There should be a registration slip for each kitten in the litter. Fill in those parts of each slip relative to sex, coat color, eye color, and (sometimes) coat length. CFA has recently requested that the breeder also stipulate if a kitten (or cat) may or may not be used for breeding.

The registration slip goes to the buyer if a kitten is sold *with papers.*

The *pedigree* is another part of a purebred's papers. (See Appendix #6 for pedigree example.) For clarity, this document should be typed. A suggestion—when preparing pedigrees, fill out all the lines on a single form except for color and sex. Make one copy for each kitten; then all you need do is add the particular color and sex.

Many times a so-called papered kitten is sold with the registration slip but without the pedigree. This happens either because the pedigree is not available or the breeder is unaware of its importance. If a pedigree is desired, a copy can generally be purchased from the association with which the kitten or its parents are registered.

A *health record*, while not necessarily a part of the papers, should be included with them. At seven to eight weeks take the kittens to the vet for examinations and first innoculations. Request individual health records stating the date and the type of immunization. If a kitten is wormed or has a physical problem, see that it is noted on its record.

Never promise a buyer that the kitten will always be well. You've bred conscientiously and done everything possible to raise a healthy pet; now it's up to the new owner to maintain that state of good health.

An *agreement of sale* (see example in Appendix #4) is imperative to avoid misunderstandings between buyer and seller. Make two copies for each kitten. Buyer and seller each sign and retain a copy.

If the kitten is to be altered, it should be sold with an *alteration agreement* (see example in Appendix #5). The same procedure is followed as with the agreement of sale.

The final item is the *instruction sheet* detailing diet and other information, such as how to groom, bathe, and discipline. It may include the due date of an immunization; a particular vitamin; a good shampoo; litter box recommendations. I like to give a personal profile of each kitten by noting its distinguishing traits, likes and dislikes, a favorite food, or a play activity that it particularly enjoys.

As a novice breeder, you may be uncertain about pricing your kittens. Ask the advice of the more experienced stud owner, or get a general idea from newspaper classifieds. As mentioned before, a kitten with papers costs more than one without, and a female is usually more expensive than a male. When fixing the price of a kitten, take into consideration its quality, personality, pedigree, and how well it conforms to breed standards.

The age at which to sell kittens varies with the breeder. Professionals and cat fanciers in the show circuit rarely sell their kittens before they reach six months of age. By that time the breeder can usually determine which ones are good enough to hold for show or for breeding. Pet quality kittens will have had all their immunizations and be ready

Flame Point Himalayan female kitten, *BR/OW/PH: Author.*

to leave. Kittens suitable to sell as breeders will have been spoken for or advertised in breeder publications.

Because beginners don't have the exposure of established breeders, they cannot avail themselves of the advantage of waiting for the kittens to develop. Homes must be found before the cuddly babies grow into the awkward stage. A need for money may be an additional pressure, as well as the fact that the newcomer faces competition from other novices who in ignorance (or desperation) will sell their purebreds at cutthroat prices.

Unless the kittens are already spoken for, I suggest that you advertise them early. Kittens of five or six weeks are at their most irresistible. They're far too young to leave their mother, but not too young to be shown to prospective new parents. As a rule, kittens may go to their new homes by ten or twelve weeks of age if they have no health problems, and if they are eating well and using the box.

When you advertise, include the words "deposits being taken." This informs the kitten-seeker that the babies are not yet old enough to leave. Or say something like "make your selection now" to indicate their tender age.

Important. If people come to look, tell them that the kittens, being so young, have not yet been immunized, and for their protection it is necessary for visitors to wash their hands (or to use a spray bottle of Nolvasan solution). This precaution is especially urgent if the visitor already owns cats or has been looking at other kittens. Disease and fungi, in particular ringworm, can unknowingly be transmitted through the human touch.

Taking a deposit on a young kitten carries advantages for both buyer and seller. It allows the purchaser time to plan for the new family member, to shop for necessities, to find a good vet, to conjecture on a name. If finances are temporarily strained, the buyer needs only to make a deposit; additional time is available to accumulate the balance. It's reassuring for the breeder to have already sold a kitten, and comforting to know that a caring home has been found.

Of even greater significance, adoption at an early age gives kitten and new owner an opportunity to get to know one another. As the breeder, you should encourage frequent visits. In addition, allow the visitor privacy so that kitten and human can learn to communicate without the reassuring familiarity of your presence.

Granted, such visits will take up valuable time, but they are well worth the sacrifice. When the day comes for that kitten to leave the only home it has known, the break won't be nearly as wrenching because it has already bonded with Its Person.

Advertising Basics

Where to advertise? Everywhere!

Put notices in your vet's office, in your car window, in supermarkets. Ask relatives and friends to tell their relatives and friends. Place classifieds in newspapers, and don't forget the freebies and the local flyers.

As this will be your first contact with prospective buyers, take the time to compose an appealing advertisement. Avoid overused adjectives such as "cute, fluffy, adorable"; in their place try nouns like "people-puss, heartwarmer, bundle of bounce." Dare to be different—it's the unique that catches the reader's eye.

Specifying the registry in an ad is debatable. Complete names are too long and most people are unfamiliar with abbreviations (except CFA). It is simpler to merely say "registered."

"Healthy" and "immunized" are important words to buyers. "Champion-sired," "loving disposition," "sweet personality" (please! not purrsonality), "home-raised," or "quality kittens" are common expressions but acceptable. Stipulate price but allow a range, such as $175 to $225, and indicate if the price includes papers. State your phone number but *not* your address unless you want strangers popping in at an any hour of the day or night. Breed should be designated, and age, sex, and color if you wish, but remember, each word beyond a certain limit costs you money.

When you've been breeding long enough to produce show quality kittens, you'll find that the classifieds of cat magazines produce excellent results. Cat shows also make a good background against which to display feline beauty and personality.

In the long run, though, you'll discover that the best advertisement is *you*—the quality of the kittens you breed, their environment, your knowledge of the breed, your business efficiency, and the manner in which you relate to people.

The ability to relate will become apparent during the second marketing contact, the *phone query*. What you say and how you say it will influence the caller's decision about pursuing the matter.

Be pleasant when responding to a phone query and try to answer questions graciously. Make your own inquiries. Is the caller familiar with the breed? If not, describe appearance, personality, and uniqueness. What quality kitten is the caller interested in—pet, breeder, or show? If your kittens are pet quality, don't belittle them by making remarks such as, "His ears are too big for show," or "She's a little cross-eyed." Stress the good points—excellent health, loving disposition, beautiful coat, home-raised, attuned to people. One thing you should try *not* to do (and it's difficult) is talk too long, as other calls may be waiting.

Every breeder can expect a number of odd telephone experiences. Selling pets seems to be different from selling anything else. You'll get every kind of call imaginable. Some people will want a specific coat color or eye color or body type, a flat nose or a long nose or no nose. Some are interested solely in price and will try to bargain. You'll hear from lonely people who only want someone to talk to. Breeders will phone to covertly test the market.

Perhaps the most frequent callers will be ordinary cat owners giving lengthy dissertations on their extraordinary felines, or asking questions only a vet could answer. Try to be patient with everyone. Not only is it rude to be curt with people but kitten buyers have been known to lurk behind the least promising of inquiries.

In due time you will learn how to effectively screen calls by careful attention to the person's voice and word choice, as well as the background sounds.

American Shorthair Kittens—*BR/OW/PH: Cherise Jolley.*

To Show and Go

If a phone query sounds favorable (or if asked) invite the caller to come and see the kittens. The *personal visit* is the third contact and the most difficult to establish. Numerous people will phone; few will come. Early in breeding I discovered that it was up to me to motivate the caller to turn off the TV, slide into the car, and drive to my home. Once I succeeded in getting a prospect through the front door, the kittens sold themselves.

When making an appointment, give explicit street directions, and just as important, allow yourself ample time to prepare. It's highly unlikely that a visitor will white-glove your coffee table, but a first impression should be one of neatness. With this in mind, I do such things as fold newspapers, empty trash, rinse the dishes in the sink. I make sure the litter boxes are clean and the premises odor free. Nothing turns off a potential pet buyer more quickly than a smelly house.

In grooming the kittens, give special attention to eyes and bottoms, and pat a little talcum powder into fuzzy coats for that sweet baby smell. As most buyers like to see the parents, groom the dam and if the sire is not available, display his picture. Check through the kittens' papers, and to induce positive thoughts, place a receipt book beside them.

Once the caller arrives, I like to chat a bit to become acquainted. Then I escort my visitor to the room where the kittens are kept. Some breeders prefer not to do it this way; instead they bring one or two kittens at a time *from* their room *to* the caller. This practice may have its advantages, but I'm always a bit suspicious of the breeder who avoids showing kittens in their own environment.

Try to time it so that the kittens are not sleeping or eating but at their liveliest. Present each kitten separately. Define sex, color, and (occasionally) temperament. Never hurry a prospect but allow latitude to hold, observe, and assess the kittens individually.

Some people know exactly what they're looking for—the eye color, coat color, sex, and personality. Others don't have a clue. All they want is a pedigreed kitten, cute, clean, loving, and in good health.

If a buyer is debating between two particular kittens, put aside the others so they won't be a distraction. Seldom should differences between kittens be discussed or one favored over another. Allow the interested party to personally discover the special qualities of each kitten and make a choice accordingly.

As a rule, stick to your price. Occasionally a buyer may want two kittens, in which instance a discount may be allowed. The advantages of a double sale and littermates remaining together far outweigh a small profit loss.

The Papers

The business end of a sale is best handled in a different setting, such as the living room or the kitchen. Talking formal matters over a cup of coffee leads to a more informal and therefore more friendly relationship.

Tactfully impress on the buyer the importance of thoroughly reading the agreement of sale before signing it. As you chat, stress such points as keeping the kitten inside the home, maintaining a proper diet, and giving immunizations and boosters as programmed. This is the time for buyer and seller to air questions or doubts and arrive at a thorough understanding of what each expects of the other.

When showing the papers, think back to the first time you tried to fill out a registration slip—you hadn't the faintest idea what went where, right? And your initial glimpse of a pedigree left you utterly bewildered by the maze of names, numbers, and abbreviations. Like as not, your new kitten owner is in the same fix and would welcome your help.

Explain how to register the kitten by writing a first and a second choice of names in the appropriate spaces of the slip. Point out information on the reverse side, such as the address and the cost. Inform the buyer that in two to four weeks a confirmation slip will be received, stating the kitten's registered name and number.

Application to register can be done at any time. Unless a name has already been chosen, you might advise the buyer to wait awhile in order to become familiar with the kitten's personality.

The neophyte kitten buyer will find the pedigree easier to understand if you characterize it as the family tree and take the time to describe its branches.

Example: "Avalon's Romeo of Highglen," the kitten's sire. Explain that "Avalon" is the first word in the sire's name because Avalon is the registered cattery where Romeo was bred. The second word, "Romeo," is the sire's given name. The next phrase, "of Highglen," means that Highglen is the name of the cattery that bought and presently owns the sire.

Your queen was purchased from a cattery registered as Rajapur; therefore, "Rajapur" precedes the name you gave her. Since, as yet, you have no registered cattery, nothing follows the given name of your queen. If eventually you decide on a cattery name, the registry, for a small fee, will add that name to your queen's pedigree.

The sire and his ancestors always occupy the top of the family tree; the dam and hers the bottom. Registration number, color, and (usually) owner are indicated for the sire and the dam. Moving to the right across the document, the known ancestors are listed, customarily going back four or five generations. Beyond five generations data is difficult to trace and is therefore unreliable.

If the family tree has the good fortune to be adorned with champions or grand champions, the titles precede the names. Titles are usually abbreviated, such as CH for champion and GC for grand champion.

The final paper is the instruction sheet. Go through it with the buyer in order to clarify any misunderstanding.

Certain cat food suppliers offer such breeder services as free "Kitten Starter Kits" (see Appendix #7 for listings). These kits are passed on to the buyer to use as files for the kitten's papers.

The majority of your purchasers will pay by personal check. Unless you know the party well, ask for one or two IDs. If papers are involved, you have the option of holding them until the check clears or turning them over with the kitten.

When taking a deposit on a kitten, give a receipt for the amount paid and *specify the balance due.* Consult with the buyer as to a favorable date for pickup and final payment. Upon mutual agreement, write the pickup date into the agreement of sale, along with a clause stating that failure to meet the time limit will result in loss of deposit.

If this last seems severe, let me tell you of an experience I had when, new at breeding, I held a kitten on a $15 deposit for three months. During that period I paid out in food, tests, and immunizations half the kitten's total cost. Then the buyer returned from a European tour and phoned to tell me that she had decided against having a pet, but out of the goodness of her heart, she would allow me to keep the deposit!

I could have sold that kitten five times over. I did not. Every breeder should exercise a code of ethics, I told myself. If a deposit is made on a kitten, you do not sell it to somebody else.

Right. But every breeder should also exercise common sense. Give the buyer a specific period of time to complete the payment and take the kitten. *Get it in writing.*

In this same context, never promise to *hold* a kitten until a phone caller arrives.

A litter record (example in Appendix #8) is an integral part of any cattery operation. In addition to listing the name, address, and phone number of each kitten buyer, it gives pricing and immunization details as well as information on the sire and the dam.

To serve as a financial statement for personal and tax purposes, the breeder should also keep a ledger, accurately reporting monthly income, expenses, and overhead.

The Followup

Once a kitten goes to its new home, the attitude of buyer toward breeder varies widely.

Some clients studiously avoid any further contact, possibly because they prefer to raise the kitten according to their own precepts. Or perhaps they look on buying a pet as a business deal, which when finished, is finished.

After several weeks, if you've heard nothing, good or bad, from a buyer, telephone to ask how the kitten is doing and if there are any problems. In about a month, for your own peace of mind, request a personal visit. Then, unless you find something amiss or the owner warms up to you, leave it alone.

Another type of kitten-buyer will call frequently to wax ecstatic over the new family member and go into great detail on its adorable habits and how much it is loved. Listen and be grateful; this is the kind of client you rarely need worry about.

Inexperienced kitten owners may call a breeder repeatedly (at least for the first several weeks). Concerned about the health and welfare of their tiny charges, they worry about every small occurrence. *Fluffy sleeps so much—is she sick? Mikey still won't let me comb him; what do I do? Jennifer sneezed twice today—should I take her to the vet?*

No matter how trivial the question, keep in mind that to the asker the problem is real. Be caring, not callous, and if you don't have a solution, suggest that a vet be consulted.

Breeders can establish warm relationships with their buyers in a number of thoughtful ways.

Slip into the kitten kit pictures of the sire and the dam, along with a few of the kittens romping through the many-faceted stages of babyhood.

If a kitten has a favorite toy, make it a gift of that toy to take to its new home.

Before a kitten leaves with its new parent, take pictures of "Fur Baby and Its Person" to mail later.

When a party who has purchased one kitten returns to buy another, not only consider it a first-rate compliment, but allow a discount.

If a sale is made because of a former buyer's recommendation, show your gratitude by a personal phone call or a thank-you note.

Once in a while hold out on an especially cute kitten picture, and on the occasion of Christmas or perhaps a first birthday, send it along with an appropriate greeting to the kitten and its owner.

When visiting a kitten, take it a toy or a food treat. Snap a few pictures to send back as a memento of the occasion.

EPILOGUE

An ailurophile is a person who loves cats. I am an ailurophile, and so are you or you'd not have read this book. We've been ailurophiles since first we touched the softness of a kitten and spilled our childish excitement in shrieks of joy. As adolescents we whispered confidences into tufted ears or dripped tears on furry heads. Even as adults, we are caught up by our passion for cats.

We decorate the shelves, walls, and tables of our homes with cats. We write on stationery enhanced with feline faces, consult cat calendars, sleep on cat pillows, and pore over cat books. When the newspaper comes, we turn to the *Garfield* strip first. Passing a pet store window, we inevitably stop to wish we could adopt every kitten sitting so morosely among the dusty wood shavings. If a cat show is scheduled for our area, we count the days until we can gape at the purebreds, so beautiful and remote behind the wires of their cages.

Now we are privileged to have one of those purebreds as part of our family. Many of us are going to be content with just that. A few will join clubs and travel the show circuit—cat fanciers in the true sense of the word. Others, like myself, will focus on breeding, occasionally bringing our cats into the limelight to take advantage of the enjoyment and the excellent contacts a show affords.

Whichever road we choose to follow, our footsteps will be that much lighter because of the cat companion walking beside us.

APPENDIX #1
THE BREEDS

ABYSSINIAN. Origin Egypt or Abyssinia (Ethiopia); one of the oldest natural breeds. Active and social, with a soft, melodious voice. Small, dainty paws, long, slender legs, and a lithe, sinewy body. Head a modified wedge with a long nose, large, erect ears, and wide, almond-shaped guileless eyes. Sleek, ticked coat needs minimal grooming; copper red or ruddy brown are best-known colors. Spirited and inquisitive, the Abby seems constantly in motion, a personality facet at odds with small apartment living. Very demonstrative but demands in return admiration and attention. Not a prolific breeder; pregnancy or delivery problems may occur.

AMERICAN BOBTAIL. Origin 1960s when a short-tailed spotted tabby male of unknown Arizona parentage was bred to a Seal Point Siamese. Mellow temperament; dotes on its owner but may be aloof upon first meeting strangers. Stocky, muscular body is topped by a broad head with alert, lynx-tipped ears, a wide nose, and a strong jaw. Short, flexible tail, either knotted or slightly curved. Toe tufts desirable. Although thick and shaggy, the double coat is nonmatting. Male is large and heavy, with a broad chest and full cheeks; rarely marks territories. Enjoys games and is good with dogs and children. Excellent breeder.

Bobkins Bow, American Bobtail, Brown Tabby male—*BR: Marlynn Claar; OW/PH: Alain Guillerme.*

Buddy, American Bobtail, White male— *BR/OW/PH: Lisa Black.*

AMERICAN CURL. Developed from a long-haired black stray with curled ears who in 1981 adopted a family in California. Her first kittens included ones with similarly curled ears, resulting in a unique breed that caused a stir in the cat fancy. The unusually shaped ears curve gently back from the face toward the center of the head, imparting an elfin charm. A moderately long, silky coat lies flat to the body with a sparsity of undercoat, thus minimal grooming. A shorthaired Curl is being developed. With a fondness for nuzzling and shoulder-riding, the Curl is a family cat, sweet, gentle, fond of children, and home-oriented.

GC & GP Katzenburg George M.P. **Washington,** American Shorthair, Silver Tabby neuter — *BR/OW/PH: Ingeborg Urcia.*

AMERICAN SHORTHAIR. Descended from the domestic cats that emigrated from Europe to America. Sturdy and solid, with broad shoulders and chest, powerful legs, and strong paws. A pleasantly open face, plump-cheeked and bright-eyed, with a medium to short nose, square muzzle, and widely spaced ears. Thick, hard coat comes in a profusion of colors and patterns; requires minimal care. Enjoys eating and is rarely choosey. Attaches itself to family and home but needs room for its frequent explosions of energy. An excellent breeder, producing four or more husky kittens in a litter.

AMERICAN WIREHAIR. Developed from a male kitten with lamblike fur found among domestic kittens on a farm in Verona, New York, 1966. Well-rounded body, round head with full cheeks, slightly curved nose, and huge, innocent eyes. Extremely dense, crimped coat, coarse on body, downy on chin and underbelly; colors and patterns run the gamut. Amicable, healthy, and long-lived. Accommodates to other felines if it can have the role of "top cat." Rare and costly.

BALINESE. Evolved in the 1950s from Siamese kittens born with long fur. Originally called Longhaired Siamese, name was later changed to Balinese because their graceful movements were reminiscent of Balinese dancers. Well-balanced, with a slim body, plumed tail, and wedge head; eyes are a deep, rich blue. Semi-long, silky, close-fitting coat with large points against pale fur; moderate grooming. An extremely high energy level bodily and vocally. Early maturity. Both sexes make excellent parents who enjoy playing with their kittens.

BENGAL. Origin USA, 1963. A cross between the Asian leopard cat and the domestic cat. Big and muscular; 10 to 22 pounds. Exquisite, plush coat with

Bengal Leopard, female—*BR/ OW/PH: Terri Pattison.*

Bengal Marble, male—*BR/OW/ PH: Terri Pattison.*

horizontal pattern of black or brown spots against beige or orange; also Snow Leopard and Marble patterns. Almond-shaped, green eyes, alert, pointed ears, and black-tipped tail carry through the jungle look. Outgoing, intelligent, active, affectionate. Loves to climb and likes water.

BIRMAN. A natural breed originating in the temples of Burma. Friendly, gentle, and appreciative of an inside environment. Good-sized, with a heavy-boned, sturdy body, bushy tail, and thick legs. Strikingly marked with dark points against a light coat that comes in a wide sweep of colors; paws are white and hind legs wear white laces. Wide, soulful, sapphire blue eyes in a round face. Pleasant, chirpy voice. An excellent breeder.

BOMBAY. Origin America. A cross between a Black American Shorthair and a Sable Burmese. Named for Bombay, India, because of its resemblance to India's black leopard. Striking appearance; glossy, jet-black coat on a supple, well-muscled body. Brilliant eyes of gold or copper. A companion cat, soft-voiced and docile, craving a serene home and a loving owner. Good breeder; kittens are born fairly light, slowly becoming completely black.

GC Pleasantview McPorkchop, Blue Point male Birman, *BR/OW/PH: Julie Collin.*

BRITISH SHORTHAIR. Origin England (possibly brought by invading Romans). Gentle, calm, friendly. A cat of ample proportions but well-balanced, with a medium to large body, thick neck, and massive head. Charming face with full cheeks, medium broad nose, and large, wide-set eyes, usually copper or orange. Dense, plush coat comes in a variety of patterns and colors, the most familiar being the solid blue. Adapts well to a roomy apartment. Not particularly a lap cat but will sit contentedly beside humans. Likes children and dogs, and breeds well. Moderate grooming.

BURMESE. Legend places it as a divinity in ancient Buddhist monasteries. Kittenish, energetic, fond of people. Compact, well-rounded body, well-muscled, with substantial bone structure. Round, golden eyes set wide apart in a full face. Short, satiny, easy-care coat. Sable brown best-known color; nonsables are often called Malayans. Likes to travel and adapts well to most environments. Garrulous by nature and enjoys long, loud conversations with owner. Healthy, long-lived, and an excellent breeder.

CHARTREUX. Bred by Carthusian monks in French monasteries as far back as the sixteenth century. Stocky, powerful build boasting a deep chest and broad shoulders. Rounded head with high-set ears, copper to gold eyes, heavy jowls, and a smiling expression. Dense, wooly, blue-grey coat is water repellent; moderate care. Very agile despite its bulk and extremely intelligent. Amiable disposition; purrs often, meows rarely.

GC DNA's Buster, Cornish Rex, Black Smoke male—BR/OW: *Diane and Alan Straka, PH: Vickie Jackson.*

COLORPOINT SHORTHAIR. Long-bodied, fine-boned, leanly muscular with long, slender legs and thin, tapering tail. Wedge-shaped head, nose long and straight, almond-shaped eyes, slightly slanted, and large, pointed ears. The soft, fine coat is easy-care and comes in a wide range of colors.

CORNISH REX. Origin Cornwall, England, 1950. Perky, gregarious. Slender, fine-boned body with long, straight legs and a whippy tail. Large ears are set high on a triangular head, nose is Roman, oval eyes large and intense. Most colors permissible in the plush coat, which is "marcelled" in tight, uniform waves with no topcoat or guardhairs. Does not shed, therefore minimal grooming. Excellent apartment cat, family-loving, intelligent, and basically healthy. Must be bred true to preserve distinctive qualities.

CYMRIC (pronounced *kim-rik*). Origin of this longhaired, tailless relative of the Manx is uncertain; could be the Isle of Man or possibly Wales, as *Cymric* is another name for *Welsh*. Appeared among normal Manx litters in Canada in the 1960s. Firm, full-chested body with a broad head, plump cheeks, a strong chin, and round, tufted ears. The medium to long coat has a heavy undercoat and a biblike ruff; although thick, the fur rarely mats. An extremely intelligent breed with an almost doglike personality; learns tricks readily, retrieves, and is home and family oriented. Breeding may be difficult.

DEVON REX. Origin Devon county in England ten years after the Cornish Rex. A clever extrovert with a pixielike appearance. Extremely large, wide ears on a triangular head; shorter nose and fuller cheeks than the Cornish Rex. Soft, curly coat with a wavy effect; wide range of colors and patterns. Slender, long-legged body is hard and muscular, tail well furred. Playful, sometimes mischievous, and devoted to family.

MGC Temek's Sitamon, Silver Egyptian Mau female. *BR/OW: Tobe Goldman, PH: David Eckard.*

EGYPTIAN MAU. Origin ancient Egypt; possibly the oldest known breed, and the only naturally spotted one. *Mau* means *cat* in ancient Egyptian tongue. Elegant, graceful, somewhat aloof, and highly intelligent. Fine, silky coat, randomly spotted on a background of silver, bronze, or smoke; banded legs and tail and one or more broken necklaces under the chin. Distinctive marking of an Egyptian scarab, or beetle, between the ears, with the scarab's head facing the tail. Large, expressive eyes of gooseberry green, slightly slanted, and emphasized with mascaralike markings. A sweet, birdlike voice and a fondness for warmth and serenity make the Egyptian an ideal inside cat. Kittens are carried 65–72 days. Good breeders.

EXOTIC SHORTHAIR. Developed in the 1960s primarily from Persians and American Shorthairs. Heavy-boned, cobby body with a bushy, abbreviated tail, short, thick legs, and large feet. Broad head has plump cheeks, button nose, low-set ears, and a "smiley" mouth. Dense, nontangling, bouncy coat, wide range of colors and patterns; eye color conforms to coat. Sometimes referred to as "a Persian in its underwear." Sweet, responsive, and quiet – a lap-cat, at ease in small quarters and tied to home and family. If kept indoors, has a life expectancy of 18–20 years.

HAVANA BROWN. Slender, green-eyed hybrid; English origin. Name derived (supposedly) from its mahogany coat color, which resembles the color of a Cuban tobacco. Spirited and playful; has a whimsical habit of picking up

SGC Cakebread's Chardonnay, Exotic Shorthair, Cream Classic Tabby female—*BR/OW: Paul & Anna Bookbinder, PH: Keith Bookbinder.*

GP & CH LaTurbie's Mitzee-Toi of Rajapur, Himalayan Tortie Point female—*BR: Helen Benge, OW/PH: Author.*

objects with its paws to investigate. An excellent apartment cat with a tendency to devote itself to an individual rather than a family. Minimal grooming. Good breeder and mother.

HIMALAYAN. Origin England and America about 1924. Loving, lively, and good-natured. Said to be the fastest-growing breed in the world. Cobby body, large head, and long flowing coat of the Persian; points and china-blue eyes of the Siamese. Adapts readily to most environments. Sweet, chirpy voice. Maximum grooming. Good breeder and has picture-book kittens.

GC Bassetti's Saisho, D.M. Japanese Bobtail, Red & White Van odd-eyed male—BR/OW: *Bob & Janet Bassetti,* PH: *Janet Bassetti.*

JAPANESE BOBTAIL. Legend places it as far back as the seventh century, when only Japanese nobility owned it. Excellent family pet, bright, happy, inquisitive. Medium-sized, fine-boned body set on long, oval-pawed legs, with rear legs longer than forelegs. Silky, medium-length fur, relatively non-shedding; the tricolor pattern (*mi-ke*) of a white coat with black and red patches thought to be especially lucky. Trademark the tail, which resembles a miniature pompon. A good traveler and a jaunty companion. Fine breeder.

KASHMIR. Himalayan in type except eyes are copper and the long coat solid chocolate or lilac with no contrasting points. In CFA classified as a solid Himalayan. Maximum grooming.

KORAT. One of the oldest natural breeds. Indigenous to Thailand where it is a good luck cat. Intelligent, loving, responsive. Huge, luminous green or amber eyes set in a heart-shaped face. Firm, muscular body clasped by a glossy silvery-blue coat; easy care. Prefers a quiet one-cat home among calm, soft-voiced humans. Good breeder.

MAINE COON. A natural breed; origin New England and Northeast Canada. One of the largest purebreds, heavy-boned and broad-chested, with sturdy legs and a long, flowing tail. Dense, shaggy, nonmatting coat in solid, shaded, or tabby colors. Big paws, heavily tufted for snow travel. High cheekbones,

SGC Shirecats Coonsbarrie Dann, Maine Coon, Brown Classic Tabby neuter—BR: *Todd & Cheri Glosier,* All My Kittens Bowdrie Jackson, Maine Coon, Classic Tabby w/White neuter—BR: *Peter Renteria,* OW: *Michael & Elizabeth Bannenberger,* PH: *Olin Mills.*

strong muzzle, large, tufted ears. Intersperses purring with distinctive trilling chirps. Home-loving but needs space. Has small litters; kittens are sometimes slow in developing.

MANX. A natural breed; origin the Isle of Man in the Irish Sea. Healthy, bright, genial. Round appearance with a high, abbreviated back and a broad chest. Short, double coat comes in a variety of colors; moderate care. Classified into three types: the *Rumpy* with no tail; the *Rumpy-rise* with a tiny stub tail; the *Longy* with a short tail. Home and people-loving. Difficult to breed perfect specimens.

NORWEGIAN FOREST CAT. A very old breed, appearing in Norse mythology. Called the Skaukatt in its homeland. First breeding pair imported to America in late 1979. Imposing appearance—big, full-chested, heavy-boned, with a bushy, high-riding tail, magnificent double coat, and large, tufted, often lynx-tipped ears. The heavy fur and wooly undercoat are water-repellent and need less grooming than other longhairs. Huge ruff frames a strong-chinned, intelligent face lit by expressive, almond-shaped eyes. Friendly and gentle, with an innate love of people. Develops slowly; five years to acquire full maturity. Robust constitution makes for a long, healthy life. Superb breeder.

OCICAT. Named after the ocelot. An ebullient breed, origin America, early 1960s, from Siamese, Abyssinian, and American Shorthair. Medium to large with a heavy, solid body. Resembles the long-extinct Egyptian spotted fishing cat in its markings of thumbprint-shaped spots scattered across sides,

SGC Maineline's Tord, male Norwegian Forest Cat, Brown Mackerel Tabby w/White – *BR/OW: Steve & Louise Clair, PH: Tetsu Yamazaki.*

shoulders, and hindquarters. Short, smoooth, close-fitting fur makes for easy care. An intensely active cat but adapts well to most environments. Prolific breeder.

ORIENTAL SHORTHAIR. Origin England, 1950s. An elegant extrovert. Siamese personality and body conformation but has green eyes and no points. Coat patterns and colors are diverse. Minimal grooming. Good breeder.

PEKE-FACED PERSIAN. American origin. Extremely flat face, wrinkled muzzle, very short, pushed-in nose, high-set ears. Cobby body, red or red tabby in color; coat long and richly full, requiring maximum care. Teeth and lower jaw may sometimes be deformed. Difficult to breed.

PERSIAN. A natural breed; the aristocrat of purebreds. Mellow, sociable, and quiet. Large, round head, strong chin, short, snub nose with deep break, and small, well-rounded ears. Huge, wide-set eyes are usually orange-gold but may be blue or green. Cobby, low-slung body set on short, sturdy legs; fluffy brush tail. An almost-nonexistent neck is adorned by an immense ruff, and long tufts of hair spring from ears and feet. Silky coat is seen in a broad spectrum of colors and patterns and requires daily grooming. Sometimes complications in breeding; kittens may be delicate.

RAGDOLL. Origin America. So called because when picked up, it is said to go limp like a rag doll. Gentle, quiet, people-loving. Large and heavy-boned, weighing 15 to 20 pounds. Long, soft, silky coat; minimal shedding. Three

GotTheLook Trick or Treat and Mardi Gras, Persian Calico kittens— *BR/OW/PH: Cherie Lightner.*

GC Katzenburg's Bismark of Katzenliebe, Russian Blue male— *BR: Ingeborg Urcia, OW/PH: Brigitte Wade.*

divisions: bicolor, colorpoint, or mitted like the Birman. Sweet face with lovely blue eyes. Can be easily hurt by children or other animals because of its trusting nature. Exclusively an indoor cat; needs a gentle owner.

RUSSIAN BLUE. Indigenous to Northern Russia and once known by names like Archangel and Maltese Blue. A natural breed, sensitive, dignified, and extremely intelligent. Large, upright ears; brilliant green eyes; often wears a "smiling" expression. Short, plush, double coat stands away from the body; the deep even blue has a silver sheen because of silver-tipped guardhairs. Reserved with strangers and disliking noise, the Blue bonds closely with its owner. A hardy breed with no major health problems. Its soft, pleasant voice

GC Shadyshack's Rocky Road, Scottish Fold, Silver Tabby w/White male – BR/OW: *Bob & Linda Rader, PH: Mark McCullough.*

CH Gotier Gelene Chatte De Mon Coeur, Siamese Seal Point female and **Gotier Gigi,** Siamese Lilac Point female – BR/OW: *Henri Pelletier/John Goterch, PH: Henri Pelletier.*

and meticulous habits make it especially suitable for apartment living. Minimal grooming. Averages four sturdy kittens in a litter.

SCOTTISH FOLD. Origin Scotland, early 1960s. Sweet, calm, gentle. Medium to large size, with a round, thick appearance, and huge, expressive eyes. Short, dense coat in a broad color range; minimal care. Outstanding feature the ears, folded forward and down, giving the winsome appearance of a tight little cap. Adapts well to most environments. Apt to be a one-person cat. Average breeder; kittens may have straight or folded ears.

SIAMESE. A natural breed; origin probably Siam. Garrulous, demanding, openly affectionate, and the acme of intelligence. Fine-limbed, slender build

Starpoint's Maya Kaliostrovna, Siberian, Brown Classic Tabby w/White female, 6 months old in winter coat. Firstborn from the mating of first imports to U.S.—*BR/OW/PH: Elizabeth Terrell.*

topped by a triangular head slanting to large, pointed ears. Dazzling blue eyes, faintly tilted; sleek, pale coat with contrasting points. A dynamic, high-energy cat; may be unsuitable for apartment living. Matures early; females have almost constant heats but deliver large litters with ease. Long-lived and healthy with a love of travel, often showing a remarkable memory for people and places.

SIBERIAN. A natural survival breed from Russia, imported to the U.S. in 1990. Vibrant, intelligent, and bold, with a pleasantly melodious voice. Large, modified-wedge head, full-cheeked and strong-chinned, with expressive, yellow-green eyes. Barrel-shaped body with superb muscling on heavy bones; neck strong and thick. Matures slowly, five years the norm, with an adult weighing 13 to 26 pounds. Medium-long to long coat, at its most spectacular in winter, with a dense undercoat and lustrous sheen to the outer fur. Very few authentic representatives in America, so if interested in this affectionate, protective cat, investigate thoroughly.

SINGAPURA. A rare natural breed from Southeast Asia (Singapore), imported to the U.S. in 1975. A charmer, delightfully outgoing and sweetly affectionate. Dainty, small to medium body wears a short, satiny, ivory coat ticked with brown. With its wide green or yellow eyes, long nose, and large, pointed ears, it resembles a miniature cougar. Soft-voiced, and fond of quiet and serenity, it appreciates a caretaker of similar temperament. An excellent apartment cat.

GC Nuance's Original Design by Rimba, Singapura, Sepia Agouti female, CFA's 15th Best Cat '90/'91, CFA's Best Singapure '90/'91—*BR/OW: Marge & Bob Jackson, PH: Douglas Pollock.*

Sabertooth Sleeper of USAF, Singapura, Sepia Agouti male—*BR/OW: Douglas Pollock & Wilson Vegas, PH: Douglas Pollock.*

SNOWSHOE. A comparatively new breed, the name derived from its well-rounded white paws. Intelligent, serene, and congenial. Well-balanced muscular body, medium to large in size. General appearance is one of power and agility, with the look of a runner rather than that of a weightlifter. Short, pale coat is set off by dark points; head wedge-shaped, tail bushy. Ideally a white inverted V runs between the blue eyes. Devoted to home and family; plays fetch like a dog, and at times delightfully clownish in behavior. Moderate grooming. Average breeder.

SOMALI. Originated in the 1960s as a longhaired mutation of the Abyssinian. Large, tufted ears and dark pencil strokes above gold or green eyes distinguish a modified wedge head. Body is slim and sinewy, tail bushy and foxlike. Medium-long coat shimmers in colors of red, ruddy, blue, or fawn, ticked with contrasting color bands. A high-energy, adventurous, often mischievous extrovert; relishes being the center of attention. Favorite pastimes include shoulder-riding, lap-sitting, and bed-snuggling. Average breeder. Moderate grooming.

Magnum's O!pus Mooncharmer Sage, Snowshoe Seal & White male— *BR/OW/PH: Bonnie Butcher.*

GC Diamonddust Desert Fire, Somali Red male— *BR/ OW: Karen Stebner, PH: Carl Widmer.*

SGC Jokatta's Dartress, Sphynx White female— *BR/ OW: Joe & Kathy Speed, PH: Tetsu Yamazaki.*

SPHYNX. Origin uncertain but has been around for at least a century. Present-day Sphynx is directly descended from a litter born to a feral cat on the streets of Toronto, Canada, 1960s. Firm and muscular with a broad chest, slim neck, and pear-shaped body. Outstanding feature is its almost total lack

Fewsee Bridget & Samson, Tonkinese, Champagne Mink female & Natural Mink neuter – BR/OW/PH: *Eileen Fusci.*

of hair, a little hair being allowed on tip of tail, bridge of nose, outsides of feet, and backs of the extremely large ears. Added to the advantage of minimal grooming, the Sphynx is hypo-allergenic; thus people who have allergies to cat hair can usually tolerate the breed. Highly intelligent, playful, cuddly, and extremely loving, often described as being "part dog, part child, part monkey, and part cat."

TONKINESE. A colorful cat with a colorful personality. Indigenous to Burma and Thailand; first recognized in the 1960s when Canadian and U.S. breeders began Siamese-Burmese crosses to reproduce the breed. Almond-shaped eyes of a gemstone quality in shades ranging from aquamarine through the blue-green spectrum. Short, glossy coat displays three patterns: the solid, which is nearly all one color; the pointed; and the mink, which has darker points. Colors include champagne, platinum, blue, natural, honey, and fawn. Enjoys travel and adapts readily to environment. Extrovertive; greets guests warmly, "answers" phone, pushes TV buttons, and bonds with children, dogs, and other cats. Active, curious, and demanding, needs an owner who will tolerate its occasional mischief and loquacity.

TURKISH ANGORA. Indigenous to Ankara (Angora), Turkey. Active and vocal. Graceful, slender body with long, slim neck and tapering, plumed tail. Wedge head has large, slightly tilted eyes, a medium-long nose, and pointed, erect ears. Coat is fine and silken, with no wooly undercoat; moderate care. Traditional color solid white but other colors and patterns now acceptable; eye color may be blue, amber, or odd-eyed. This is a house cat who prefers living with one doting owner. Excellent breeder.

Lotsaluvan's Kizi Van Kedi, Turkish Van Auburn & White male—*BR/OW: Ann R. Van Brunt, PH: Mark McCullough.*

TURKISH VAN. Indigenous to the Lake Van area in Turkey. A charismatic breed, spirited and affectionate. Long-bodied, muscular, and deep-chested, with fairly long legs, large, tufted feet, and a full-brush tail. Broad wedge head has prominent cheekbones, a long nose, round amber or blue eyes, and a white blaze separating large, high-set ears that are well-feathered inside. Chalk-white coat carries markings in auburn, black, blue, cream, tortoise shell, or blue-cream, preferably on head and tail. Also acceptable are one or more random markings such as the one called the Mark of Allah, which appears between the shoulder blades. Prefers an inside environment with a doting human. Has an unusual affinity for water; coat is practically waterproof because of a singular cashmerelike texture. A strong, healthy breed, taking three to five years to mature. Asks for minimal grooming, maximum affection.

Note: Some breeds may not yet be recognized for championship status.

APPENDIX #2
CAT ASSOCIATIONS (as of 1992)

American Cat Association (ACA) *(Regional)*
Oldest U.S.A. registry
8101 Katherine Avenue
Panorama City, CA 91402

American Cat Council (ACC) *(Regional)*
P. O. Box 626
Pasadena, CA 91102

American Cat Fanciers' Association (ACFA) *(National and International)*
Founded 1955
P. O. Box 203
Point Lookout, MO 65726

Canadian Cat Association (CCA)
83 Kennedy Rd., Unit 1806
Brampton, Ontario, Canada L6W 3P3

Cat Fanciers' Association, Inc. (CFA) (National and International)
Founded 1906
1805 Atlantic Avenue
P. O. Box 1005
Manasquan, NJ 08736-0805

Cat Fanciers' Federation, Inc. (CFF) (National and International)
Founded 1919
9509 Montgomery Road
Cincinnati, OH 45242

Crown Cat Fanciers' Federation (CCFF) (Regional)
P. O. Box 34
Nazareth, KY 40048

The International Cat Association (TICA) (National and International)
Founded 1979
P. O. Box 2684
Harlingen, TX 78551

APPENDIX #3A
STUD SERVICE AGREEMENT A

I, _____, owner of

_____ ,

(breed) _____ (color) _____ ,

promise to pay to _____ ,

owner of _____ ,

(breed) _____ (color) _____ ,

the sum of $_____ (_____ dollars)

for service to the above queen. The fee is to be paid as follows: a deposit

of $_____ and the balance of $_____ four weeks from the first day of visit.
Upon receipt of the final payment, the stud's owner will give the queen's owner
a copy of the stud's pedigree and a signed Litter Registration Application to
indicate fulfillment of contract. If no pregnancy results from the initial meeting,
the stud owner guarantees two return services at no extra cost.

SOLE RESPONSIBILITY OF THE ABOVE NAMED STUD IS TO IM-
PREGNATE THE ABOVE NAMED QUEEN. HE HAS NO RESPON-
SIBILITY REGARDING THE NUMBER, SEX, OR SURVIVAL OF THE
RESULTING KITTENS.

Date _____

_____   _____
Queen's Owner   Stud's Owner

APPENDIX #3B
STUD SERVICE AGREEMENT B

Name of stud _____

CFA # _____ Breed _____ Color _____

Name of queen _____

CFA # _____ Breed _____ Color _____

    The owner of the above queen agrees to pay the owner of the above stud
a service fee of $_____ OR one (pick of the litter) kitten resulting from
the mating of the above queen to the above stud.
    The stud owner may visit the kittens when they are approximately six
weeks of age. If the stud owner opts for a kitten, said kitten will be released
upon request, providing it is no younger than eight weeks and no older than
fourteen. The queen's owner will furnish proof of a negative FeLV test and
a first immunization on said kitten.
    If the stud owner opts for a monetary fee, said fee is due two weeks from
the date of option. Upon receipt of either kitten or fee, the stud owner will
provide a copy of the stud's pedigree and a signed Litter Registration form.
    If only one kitten survives, the queen's owner may retain the kitten and
pay the stud fee; or release the kitten per the agreement.
    If the initial mating proves unsuccessful, two return services are guar-
anteed. If the queen still fails to conceive, her owner will pay the stud owner
$10 per day for each day of boarding; this amount to be paid in full no later
than four weeks after final mating, and is in lieu of a kitten or a stud fee.

Date_____

_____   _____
Owner of queen   Owner of Stud

APPENDIX #3C
STUD CLIENT'S
INFORMATION SHEET

Queen's name_____ Approx. due date_____

PREGNANCY SIGNS
   Heat cycle ends
   Nipples enlarge and pinken in color
   Becomes calmer, more loving
   Appetite picks up
   Some cats have "morning sickness"
   Starts gaining weight after four weeks

     The duration of normal gestation (pregnancy) is sixty-one to sixty-seven days.

     On your vet's advice, give a vitamin/mineral supplement, in particular *calcium*.

     Serve a midday snack as well as two regular meals.

     Appetite should remain hearty until just before delivery.

     Maintain moderate exercise.

     Give extra love and attention, particularly the last two weeks.

     A prenatal veterinarian's examination two weeks before due date is optional.

     A postnatal veterinarian's examination is *vital*.

APPENDIX #4
AGREEMENT OF SALE

Buyer _____ Phone _____

Address _____

City _____ State _____ Zip _____

Seller _____ Phone _____

Address _____

City _____ State _____ Zip _____

Cat/kitten's sex _____ Color _____ Breed _____

Born _____ Litter # _____ Registration # _____

Cattery Name _____ # _____

Purchase Price _____ Date _____

   This cat/kitten has been examined by _____ D.V.M.,

and found to be in good health with no apparent genetic faults. It is free of any liens

such as stud fees or veterinary fees. Immunization(s) _____ has/have been given.

   The buyer agrees to provide proper housing, diet, and general health care, including the completion of immunizations (unless already given) plus yearly boosters. The cat/kitten is to be kept inside.

   If within 48 hours of the sale, the buyer believes the cat/kitten to be sick, the buyer will take the cat/kitten to the seller who will either refund the purchase price or return the cat/kitten in well condition. If professional medical care is given to the cat/kitten during this 48 hours, the seller is not responsible for any monies paid out by the buyer.

   Deletions or additions to this contract must be initialed by both parties. Aware that this Agreement of Sale is for mutual benefit, we hereby affix our signatures.

_____   _____
Buyer   Seller

APPENDIX #5
ALTERATION AGREEMENT

Buyer _____ Phone _____

Address _____

City _____ State _____ Zip _____

Seller _____ Phone _____

Address _____

City _____ State _____ Zip _____

Sex _____ Color _____ Breed _____ Born _____

Litter registration # _____ (or) Registration # _____

Cattery name _____ Cattery # _____

Purchase price $_____ Date _____

The buyer promises to have the above kitten altered as soon as declared old enough by a veterinarian; said altering to take place no later than _____. The buyer will remit to the seller written verification of altering within one month after the above date or be obligated for an additional payment of $_____, due immediately. The buyer further agrees to: a) keep the kitten strictly inside the home, b) give it proper diet and general health care, including immunizations and yearly boosters, c) notify the seller if the kitten is resold or given away.

The seller agrees to deliver or mail the kitten's papers to the buyer within _____ days after notification of altering.

_____   _____
Buyer   Seller

PEDIGREE

Name: **CH BANNERCRESTS MAYA OF RAJAPUR**
No.: CFA 3279-703815
Breed: HIMALAYAN
Color: FLAMEPOINT
Eye Color: BLUE
Sex: FEMALE
Born: 2/15/91
Breeder: KITTY NOWOTNEY
Owner: ELAINE GILBERTSON

Sire: CH Woodlinnd's Satin Shirt of Luvmew
No: 3278-373149
Color: Flamepoint

Dam: CH Bannercrest Peaches and Cream
No: 3279-29771
Color: Flamepoint

Sire: GRCH Sultan's Syndicate Boss
No: 3272-2682870
Color: Sealpoint

Dam: Woodlinnd's Satin Lady
No: 3289-338485
Color: Blue Creampoint

Sire: Delfa Master Joshua of Bannercrest
No: 3278-245351
Color: Flamepoint

Dam: Himmysweet's It's It of Bannercrest
No: 3293-202203
Color: Tortiepoint

DBL GRC T-Renn's Campaign of Sulltan's
172-83647 Sealpoint

CH T-Renn's Tradition
177-140164 Bluepoint

Lotsapurr Soldier Boy of Woodlinnds's
3010-248628 Red CPC

Woodlinnd's Satin Doll
3289-256930 Blue Crpt

CH Madame Nu's Gold Nugget of Delfa
178-082895 Flamepoint

CH Delfa Dew Drop
0197-166501 Creampoint

GRCH Himmysweet's Candy Man
178-112570 Flamepoint

Purzelot's Necco 2
195-141575 Tortie Hybrid CPC

T-Renn's Compani
Blue Hybrid CPC
Turxis Valley Sho-n-tel
Black Hybrid CPC

La Chateau's Indiana Jones
Bluepoint
T-Renn's Tara
Blue Hybrid CPC

Thesaurus Crescendo
Bluepoint
Lotsapurr Strike My Fancy
Red Hybrid CPC

CH Kueen Kool-Aid of Woodlinnd's
Creampoint
Surval See Me Shine of Woodlinnd's
Blue Crpt

GRCH Madame Nu's Zodiac
Bluepoint
Kyhina 18 Karat of Madame Nu
Red

Kueen Morky
Cream
CH Kueen Country Girl of Delfa
Tortiepoint

Luddington's Bartender
Black Hybrid
Bits of Honey of Himmysweet's
Blue Creampoint

Purzelot's Hot Shot
Flamepoint
Himmeden's Gwendolyn of Purzelot
Tortie Hybrid

I CERTIFY that to the best of my knowledge and belief, the above pedigree is true and correct.
Signed this _____ day of _____ 19 ___

Breeder   Cattery Name   Number

APPENDIX #7
KITTEN STARTER KITS

ANF Pet Formula
"Best of the Best Bonus Club"
P. O. Box 285
Nashville, TN 37202

Dad's Products Company, Inc.
"Kitten Starter Kits"
P. O. Box 451-D
Meadville, PA 16335

Hill's Pet Products
Science Diet Best
Breeder-Exhibitor Services Team
P. O. Box 148
Topeka, KS 66601

Iams Company
Iams Breeder Club
7250 Poe Avenue
Dayton, OH 45414

Ralston Purina Company
"Purina Pro Club"
"Purnia Pro Plan Kitten Starter Kits"
P. O. Box 7966
St. Louis, MO 63106-9925

Kal Kan Foods, Inc.
"Professional Services Program"
3250 44th Street
Vernon, CA 90058

(*Note:* As this list was compiled before the publishing date, there may be changes in addresses, companies, and programs.)

APPENDIX #8
LITTER RECORD

Litter Registration Number _____

Dam _____

Sire _____

Owner of Sire _____ Fee _____

Address _____ Phone _____

City _____ State _____ Zip _____

Date bred _____ Gestation _____ days Birth Date _____

Notes on pregnancy and parturition: _____

_____

_____

KITTENS

	Sex	Color	Alter.	Cost
1	_____	_____	_____	$ _____

(Buyer's Name) _____

(Address) _____ (Phone) _____

2 _____ _____ _____ $ _____

(Buyer's Name) _____

(Address) _____ (Phone) _____

3 _____ _____ _____ $ _____

(Buyer's Name) _____

(Address) _____ (Phone) _____

4 _____ _____ _____ $ _____

(Buyer's Name) _____

(Address) _____ (Phone) _____

IMMUNIZATIONS

Date _____ Type _____ Reaction _____

Additional notes: _____

_____

_____

APPENDIX #9
POISONOUS PLANTS

Anemone
Amaryllis
Azalea
Baneberry
Bird-of-Paradise
Black-eyed Susan
Bleeding Heart
Buttercup
Cactus
Caladium
Calla Lily
Castor Bean
Chrysanthemum
Cornflower
Creeping Charlie
Crocus
Cyclamen
Daffodil
Delphinium
Diffenbachia
Elephant Ears
Four O'Clock
Holly
Honeysuckle
Hyacinth
Hydrangea
Iris

Ivy
Jack-in-the-Pulpit
Jimson Weed
Jonquil
Lantana
Larkspur
Lily (most kinds)
Locoweed
Mistletoe
Monks Hood
Morning Glory
Narcissus
Nightshade
Oleander
Peony
Philodendron
Poinsettia
Poppy
Pothos
Schefflera
Scotch Broom
Spider Plant
Sprengeri Fern
Star-of-Bethlehem
Sweet Pea
Tulip
Wisteria

APPENDIX #10. GESTATION CHART (65 DAYS)

MATED	DUE	MATED	DUE	MATED	DUE
01–Jan	07–Mar	03–Mar	07–May	03–May	07–Jul
02–Jan	08–Mar	04–Mar	08–May	04–May	08–Jul
03–Jan	09–Mar	05–Mar	09–May	05–May	09–Jul
04–Jan	10–Mar	06–Mar	10–May	06–May	10–Jul
05–Jan	11–Mar	07–Mar	11–May	07–May	11–Jul
06–Jan	12–Mar	08–Mar	12–May	08–May	12–Jul
07–Jan	13–Mar	09–Mar	13–May	09–May	13–Jul
08–Jan	14–Mar	10–Mar	14–May	10–May	14–Jul
09–Jan	15–Mar	11–Mar	15–May	11–May	15–Jul
10–Jan	16–Mar	12–Mar	16–May	12–May	16–Jul
11–Jan	17–Mar	13–Mar	17–May	13–May	17–Jul
12–Jan	18–Mar	14–Mar	18–May	14–May	18–Jul
13–Jan	19–Mar	15–Mar	19–May	15–May	19–Jul
14–Jan	20–Mar	16–Mar	20–May	16–May	20–Jul
15–Jan	21–Mar	17–Mar	21–May	17–May	21–Jul
16–Jan	22–Mar	18–Mar	22–May	18–May	22–Jul
17–Jan	23–Mar	19–Mar	23–May	19–May	23–Jul
18–Jan	24–Mar	20–Mar	24–May	20–May	24–Jul
19–Jan	25–Mar	21–Mar	25–May	21–May	25–Jul
20–Jan	26–Mar	22–Mar	26–May	22–May	26–Jul
21–Jan	27–Mar	23–Mar	27–May	23–May	27–Jul
22–Jan	28–Mar	24–Mar	28–May	24–May	28–Jul
23–Jan	29–Mar	25–Mar	29–May	25–May	29–Jul
24–Jan	30–Mar	26–Mar	30–May	26–May	30–Jul
25–Jan	31–Mar	27–Mar	31–May	27–May	31–Jul
26–Jan	01–Apr	28–Mar	01–Jun	28–May	01–Aug
27–Jan	02–Apr	29–Mar	02–Jun	29–May	02–Aug
28–Jan	03–Apr	30–Mar	03–Jun	30–May	03–Aug
29–Jan	04–Apr	31–Mar	04–Jun	31–May	04–Aug
30–Jan	05–Apr	01–Apr	05–Jun	01–Jun	05–Aug
31–Jan	06–Apr	02–Apr	06–Jun	02–Jun	06–Aug
01–Feb	07–Apr	03–Apr	07–Jun	03–Jun	07–Aug
02–Feb	08–Apr	04–Apr	08–Jun	04–Jun	08–Aug
03–Feb	09–Apr	05–Apr	09–Jun	05–Jun	09–Aug
04–Feb	10–Apr	06–Apr	10–Jun	06–Jun	10–Aug
05–Feb	11–Apr	07–Apr	11–Jun	07–Jun	11–Aug
06–Feb	12–Apr	08–Apr	12–Jun	08–Jun	12–Aug
07–Feb	13–Apr	09–Apr	13–Jun	09–Jun	13–Aug
08–Feb	14–Apr	10–Apr	14–Jun	10–Jun	14–Aug
09–Feb	15–Apr	11–Apr	15–Jun	11–Jun	15–Aug
10–Feb	16–Apr	12–Apr	16–Jun	12–Jun	16–Aug
11–Feb	17–Apr	13–Apr	17–Jun	13–Jun	17–Aug
12–Feb	18–Apr	14–Apr	18–Jun	14–Jun	18–Aug
13–Feb	19–Apr	15–Apr	19–Jun	15–Jun	19–Aug
14–Feb	20–Apr	16–Apr	20–Jun	16–Jun	20–Aug
15–Feb	21–Apr	17–Apr	21–Jun	17–Jun	21–Aug
16–Feb	22–Apr	18–Apr	22–Jun	18–Jun	22–Aug
17–Feb	23–Apr	19–Apr	23–Jun	19–Jun	23–Aug
18–Feb	24–Apr	20–Apr	24–Jun	20–Jun	24–Aug
19–Feb	25–Apr	21–Apr	25–Jun	21–Jun	25–Aug
20–Feb	26–Apr	22–Apr	26–Jun	22–Jun	26–Aug
21–Feb	27–Apr	23–Apr	27–Jun	23–Jun	27–Aug
22–Feb	28–Apr	24–Apr	28–Jun	24–Jun	28–Aug
23–Feb	29–Apr	25–Apr	29–Jun	25–Jun	29–Aug
24–Feb	30–Apr	26–Apr	30–Jun	26–Jun	30–Aug
25–Feb	01–May	27–Apr	01–Jul	27–Jun	31–Aug
26–Feb	02–May	28–Apr	02–Jul	28–Jun	01–Sep
27–Feb	03–May	29–Apr	03–Jul	29–Jun	02–Sep
28–Feb	04–May	30–Apr	04–Jul	30–Jun	03–Sep
01–Mar	05–May	01–May	05–Jul	01–Jul	04–Sep
02–Mar	06–May	02–May	06–Jul	02–Jul	05–Sep

**NOTE: This chart is configured as a non–leap year calendar.
From March 1 in a leap year, 1 day would need to be added to due date.**

APPENDIX #10 (Continued). GESTATION CHART (65 DAYS)

MATED	DUE	MATED	DUE	MATED	DUE
03–Jul	06–Sep	02–Sep	06–Nov	02–Nov	06–Jan
04–Jul	07–Sep	03–Sep	07–Nov	03–Nov	07–Jan
05–Jul	08–Sep	04–Sep	08–Nov	04–Nov	08–Jan
06–Jul	09–Sep	05–Sep	09–Nov	05–Nov	09–Jan
07–Jul	10–Sep	06–Sep	10–Nov	06–Nov	10–Jan
08–Jul	11–Sep	07–Sep	11–Nov	07–Nov	11–Jan
09–Jul	12–Sep	08–Sep	12–Nov	08–Nov	12–Jan
10–Jul	13–Sep	09–Sep	13–Nov	09–Nov	13–Jan
11–Jul	14–Sep	10–Sep	14–Nov	10–Nov	14–Jan
12–Jul	15–Sep	11–Sep	15–Nov	11–Nov	15–Jan
13–Jul	16–Sep	12–Sep	16–Nov	12–Nov	16–Jan
14–Jul	17–Sep	13–Sep	17–Nov	13–Nov	17–Jan
15–Jul	18–Sep	14–Sep	18–Nov	14–Nov	18–Jan
16–Jul	19–Sep	15–Sep	19–Nov	15–Nov	19–Jan
17–Jul	20–Sep	16–Sep	20–Nov	16–Nov	20–Jan
18–Jul	21–Sep	17–Sep	21–Nov	17–Nov	21–Jan
19–Jul	22–Sep	18–Sep	22–Nov	18–Nov	22–Jan
20–Jul	23–Sep	19–Sep	23–Nov	19–Nov	23–Jan
21–Jul	24–Sep	20–Sep	24–Nov	20–Nov	24–Jan
22–Jul	25–Sep	21–Sep	25–Nov	21–Nov	25–Jan
23–Jul	26–Sep	22–Sep	26–Nov	22–Nov	26–Jan
24–Jul	27–Sep	23–Sep	27–Nov	23–Nov	27–Jan
25–Jul	28–Sep	24–Sep	28–Nov	24–Nov	28–Jan
26–Jul	29–Sep	25–Sep	29–Nov	25–Nov	29–Jan
27–Jul	30–Sep	26–Sep	30–Nov	26–Nov	30–Jan
28–Jul	01–Oct	27–Sep	01–Dec	27–Nov	31–Jan
29–Jul	02–Oct	28–Sep	02–Dec	28–Nov	01–Feb
30–Jul	03–Oct	29–Sep	03–Dec	29–Nov	02–Feb
31–Jul	04–Oct	30–Sep	04–Dec	30–Nov	03–Feb
01–Aug	05–Oct	01–Oct	05–Dec	01–Dec	04–Feb
02–Aug	06–Oct	02–Oct	06–Dec	02–Dec	05–Feb
03–Aug	07–Oct	03–Oct	07–Dec	03–Dec	06–Feb
04–Aug	08–Oct	04–Oct	08–Dec	04–Dec	07–Feb
05–Aug	09–Oct	05–Oct	09–Dec	05–Dec	08–Feb
06–Aug	10–Oct	06–Oct	10–Dec	06–Dec	09–Feb
07–Aug	11–Oct	07–Oct	11–Dec	07–Dec	10–Feb
08–Aug	12–Oct	08–Oct	12–Dec	08–Dec	11–Feb
09–Aug	13–Oct	09–Oct	13–Dec	09–Dec	12–Feb
10–Aug	14–Oct	10–Oct	14–Dec	10–Dec	13–Feb
11–Aug	15–Oct	11–Oct	15–Dec	11–Dec	14–Feb
12–Aug	16–Oct	12–Oct	16–Dec	12–Dec	15–Feb
13–Aug	17–Oct	13–Oct	17–Dec	13–Dec	16–Feb
14–Aug	18–Oct	14–Oct	18–Dec	14–Dec	17–Feb
15–Aug	19–Oct	15–Oct	19–Dec	15–Dec	18–Feb
16–Aug	20–Oct	16–Oct	20–Dec	16–Dec	19–Feb
17–Aug	21–Oct	17–Oct	21–Dec	17–Dec	20–Feb
18–Aug	22–Oct	18–Oct	22–Dec	18–Dec	21–Feb
19–Aug	23–Oct	19–Oct	23–Dec	19–Dec	22–Feb
20–Aug	24–Oct	20–Oct	24–Dec	20–Dec	23–Feb
21–Aug	25–Oct	21–Oct	25–Dec	21–Dec	24–Feb
22–Aug	26–Oct	22–Oct	26–Dec	22–Dec	25–Feb
23–Aug	27–Oct	23–Oct	27–Dec	23–Dec	26–Feb
24–Aug	28–Oct	24–Oct	28–Dec	24–Dec	27–Feb
25–Aug	29–Oct	25–Oct	29–Dec	25–Dec	28–Feb
26–Aug	30–Oct	26–Oct	30–Dec	26–Dec	01–Mar
27–Aug	31–Oct	27–Oct	31–Dec	27–Dec	02–Mar
28–Aug	01–Nov	28–Oct	01–Jan	28–Dec	03–Mar
29–Aug	02–Nov	29–Oct	02–Jan	29–Dec	04–Mar
30–Aug	03–Nov	30–Oct	03–Jan	30–Dec	05–Mar
31–Aug	04–Nov	31–Oct	04–Jan	31–Dec	06–Mar
01–Sep	05–Nov	01–Nov	05–Jan		

NOTE: This chart is configured as a non–leap year calendar.
From March 1 in a leap year, 1 day would need to be added to due date.

TIPS

Cleaning

Important. Clean a stain immediately. If you don't, it will smell, be more difficult to remove, and may encourage repeat offenses.

Use a dustpan to pick up solid feces or a furball; it eliminates handling, and rinses clean in a jiffy.

Baking soda will deodorize carpets or upholstery.

Bleach is the most effective and the cheapest disinfectant. For normal cleaning use four ounces to a gallon of water and rinse well. To disinfect, use concentrated bleach and leave on the surface for ½ hour before thorough rinsing. Do not use soap or detergents with bleach, as they reduce the action.

Never use a cleaner made with phenol or carbolic acid; they may be poisonous to a cat.

For a linoleum or tile floor, use a dust mop to swish together spilled litter, fur, food, and the like. Then pick up with a hand vacuum. Occasionally machine-wash the mop on gentle cycle and dry outside. Before reusing the dust mop, renew it with a product like Endust.

A plastic spray bottle filled with a solution of a disinfectant cleaner like OdoKlean or Nolvasan simplifies the washing of tables, countertops, and walls.

For carpet or upholstery spots, first wipe as dry as possible with a paper towel or a cloth. Then try either 1) club soda, 2) white vinegar, 3) Seven-Up, 4) baking soda. Test first on a small area.

Lightly spray water on fabric where hair has collected, then roll with your fingers or use a brush to collect.

To collect hair from carpeting, try a squeegee.

Feeding

If you prefer a ceramic feeding bowl, be sure it is American-made. Imported ceramics often have not been sufficiently kiln-fired, thus allowing the poisonous lead content of the glaze to leach through.

Corn oil supplies essential fatty acids and is an excellent source of vitamin E.

Add zest to food by sprinkling it with grated cheddar cheese.

If you are concerned over possible salmonella bacteria in raw eggs, either cook them or pour boiling water over them while still in the shell.

Fleas

Before vacuuming, put a flea collar or mothballs inside the vacuum bag to kill the fleas you sweep up.

Add a little liquid flea killer to rug shampoo before cleaning. Test on a small area first.

Place a cut-up flea collar under your cat's bedding.

Punch holes in the lid of a clean empty glass jar and fill with 20 Mule Team Borax. Sprinkle on furniture, carpet, and your cat's bed. Leave on for several hours or an entire day before vacuuming. Repeat a week later or for as long as the flea problem exists. Borax dries out flea eggs, thus stopping reproduction.

Finally! A safe deterrent for fleas on newborn kittens. Twice daily rub into their skin water-diluted Avon Skin So Soft Bath Oil. Or try a sprinkle of garlic powder on their backs; if the mother cat licks it off, it won't hurt her.

If you insist that your cat wear a flea collar, these suggestions are offered: Leave a new flea collar exposed to the air (in a safe place) for several days before putting it on your cat. Watch your feline for grogginess, red eyes, runny nose, or skin inflammation. If any of these symptoms develop, remove the collar immediately.

A wet flea collar doesn't work and may become toxic.

Cats sometimes have a reaction to the pyrethrin in flea sprays. Symptoms include drooling, excitement, or depression. If this occurs, quickly rinse the cat with warm water to allay the reaction, then notify your vet.

Immediately after flea-spraying a cat, wrap it in a towel with only its head sticking out; keep it wrapped for about ten minutes. This may prevent a reaction from inhaling the fumes or licking the fur.

When picking off live fleas, put Vaseline on your fingertips, then scrape off the fleas into a container of hydrogen peroxide. A tweezer also makes a good flea-picker.

If you prefer the holistic approach to the flea problem, try herbs. Steep one teaspoon of rosemary in a cup of boiling water, cool and add to plain cat shampoo or use as a spray. Other flea-repelling herbs are rue, wormwood, pennyroyal, eucalyptus, and citronella. Use any of these sparingly and with caution.

A slight amount of vinegar added to a cat's drinking water is reputed to be a natural flea repellent. So is garlic, brewers yeast, kelp, or vitamin C stirred into the food. Occasionally one or the other helps—but only occasionally.

Health Problems

For nasal congestion try baby nose drops or a vaporizer.

If your cat can't eat because of a sore throat, stir a little water into strained baby food to make it slide down easier.

Tempt the appetite of a sick kitten with the salty taste of beef or chicken bouillon cubes dissolved in warm water; make the bouillon about ⅓ strength.

Nourish a sick cat by giving it Nutrical mixed with warm water until thin enough to feed with a syringe.

Eating too much cat litter may upset a kitten's tummy. To relieve, feed small amounts of sugar water with a dropper or syringe.

An adult cat who eats litter may be suffering from *pica*, a lack of vitamins or minerals. Or the cat could simply be bored.

If standard hairball medications do not help your constipated feline, try Metamucil, bran, or canned pumpkin, or a combination of the three in *small amounts*. High fiber food like Iams Less Active may also help.

If a cat drools excessively, it should be vet-checked. Causes range from bad teeth to a rodent ulcer to an upper respiratory infection. Occasionally drooling arises from simple overexcitement.

After surgery, a cat will often bite and claw at its stitches. This can be averted by an Elizabethan collar. The collar is expensive, but you can make your own from a large piece of cardboard. Cut a hole in the middle large enough for your cat's head; then cut a straight line from the outside edge to the hole. Carefully place the cardboard collar around your cat's neck and tape together the straight edges. Remove to allow eating and drinking.

To get a urine specimen, pour a small amount of cat litter into one end of a clean box. After your cat urinates, slightly tip the box, making the urine run down the slope and puddle. Draw it out with a syringe and pour it into a small bottle or vial. Write the cat's name, the owner's name, and the date on a piece of tape and attach. Refrigerate until it can be taken in for analysis. For a fecal sample, use a similar method.

FUS (Feline Urological Syndrome) is a term used for a number of illnesses associated with the urinary tract. Causes are varied and speculative. They range from obesity to neutering, indoor confinement to insufficient or dirty drinking water, cold weather to viruses, bacteria, genetics, or a lack of exercise. However, it is well proven that a diet high in alkalines and magnesium can be a factor contributing to urinary problems. Help assure your feline's good health by a thorough study of cat food labels. A litter has been invented that, by turning different colors, alerts a cat's owner to changes in the cat's urine; thus FUS can be caught in its early stages.

Do not give a cat aspirin or Tylenol; they can be deadly. Aspirin is also present in Pepto-Bismol.

Avoid shampooing your cat in dishwashing detergent or human shampoos and hand soap.

For a minor cut or abrasion, medicate with an antiseptic made for small children.

Grooming

For fur that smells of urine, rub in baking soda; then brush thoroughly.

Yellow stains on a white or pale coat can be removed by scrubbing carefully with a solution of cornstarch and hydrogen peroxide.

If your cat dislikes grooming, try storing the comb and brush in a bag with catnip.

Excessive shedding could be from a lack of fatty acid in the diet. Try a product like Linatone.

Lecithin is excellent for improving the coat of a longhair.

If your cat's hair sparks with electricity, use an antistatic coat conditioner.

A comb called the Untangler takes the ouch! out of combing longhaired cats.

Before taking your cat to the show ring, mix flea powder and baby talcum powder and apply lightly to the coat. Brush out thoroughly.

Scrape tartar from teeth with your thumbnail or a small spoon, then clean with a bit of coarse cloth moistened in a mixture of one cup water and ½ teaspoon salt.

Stud tail, which is the greasy accumulation near the top of a cat's tail, can be alleviated with ordinary kitchen cornstarch. Rub it in thoroughly; then brush. A new baby powder of 100 percent cornstarch is an alternative. Degrease the tail every day until the problem clears. You might also try washing the area with mechanic's soap during your cat's bath.

Crud chin is a type of acne often seen on white or light cats. Several times a day soften the crud with a warm, wet cloth. Comb out as much as possible and rinse. Scrub lightly with Phisohex or a similar product and again rinse well. Finally, and most importantly, dab with a cotton ball soaked in Listerine. (Some breeders use Lip Aid.)

Litter Box

For that hard, crusty buildup on sides and bottom of the box, try a product like Lime Away. Mix with hot water according to directions and soak for several hours. Rinse thoroughly.

Wrap your hand in a small plastic bag to pick up dry feces that sometimes miss the litter box. (You can use produce bags from the market.)

Various kinds of litter are offered today, including the new "scoop." This is a specially formulated cat litter that absorbs liquid waste and forms it into a scoopable clump. Solid waste is similarly coated for easy removal. Additional litter is added as needed. On a personal note, this type of box filler seems to be dustier and tracks more. Also, despite claims of its lasting for months, I find it necessary to empty, wash and refill the boxes after about six weeks of use. On the other hand, the ease, the economy, and the lack of odor, in addition to no heavy bags to lift and store, make scoop litter an undeniable plus.

Common household products like Bon Ami, Comet Cleanser, or Ivory Liquid can be used to clean the litter box.

If using clay litter, eliminate box odors by mixing in one part of baking soda to three parts of litter. Or give the box that sweet baby smell with a sprinkle of an inexpensive baby powder.

A large slotted metal spoon makes an excellent scoop for feces or scoop litter.

If you use a lidded box, put a charcoal filter under the lid to absorb odors.

Because bacteria grow rapidly on feces in the litter box, scoop it out at least twice a day.

Your cat will refuse to use the box if
  It's too dirty. Shame on you! Clean it.
  It's too clean. Sprinkle in a little used litter.
  It's too small. Get one to fit.
  It's a community pan. Supply more boxes.
  It has been cleaned with ammonia—confusing to a cat because ammonia smells like old urine.
  Your cat is bashful. Give the shy kitty privacy with a little screen, or put the box in a closet.
  It has a liner. Remove the unnecessary plastic.
  It's the wrong kind of litter. Use different ones until you find your cat's preference.

For wee kittens, start their toilet training in a lowsided box; a square metal cake tin is ideal.

When you bring home your new kitten, help it adapt to the new litter box by mixing a little of its old used litter with the fresh.

Miscellaneous

Have spray bottles of water in each room of the house, ready to startle a misbehaving feline. A whistle or a water gun are other mischief-deterrents.

Give insistent clawers a seagrass doormat or an old bathmat on which to claw.

Reasons *not* to declaw a cat:
  It weakens leg, shoulder, and back muscles.
  It takes away the sense of balance.
  It deprives a cat of self-protection.
  A declawed cat may turn to biting instead of scratching.
  It can cause infection, or permanently cripple.
  It is painful.

Before introducing a cat or a kitten into a home where other cats have established their territory, rub the body of the new feline with a small cloth to transfer its odor. Bring the cloth home to the established residents and allow them to sniff and paw at it. Repeat several times before introducing the newcomer.

Before you buy an expensive cat bed, try out a homemade one (like a cardboard box) to find out if your feline will sleep in it.

If your cat insists on sleeping with you, bring its bed into your room and place it next to yours.

Before you pick up a cat or a kitten, make a soft noise to let it know you are there.

Empty glass jars make good containers for dry cat food.

Tabasco sauce or bitter apple are excellent deterrents for the cat who chews indiscriminately.

Place your cat's bed on a level higher than the floor; it wards off drafts and gives your pet a sense of security.

Getting KMR to water-blend without lumping can be a frustrating task. Measure the proper amount into a wide-mouthed glass jar, water first. To mix, use the type of coiled stainless steel whisk that goes up and down like a spring.

GLOSSARY

ACA. American Cat Association (the oldest registry).
ACFA. American Cat Fanciers' Association.
ALTER. A term for a neutered cat.
ANESTRUS. The sexually inactive period.
BENCH. A cat show term referring to the place assigned to an entrant.
BENCHED. Meaning the cat is present and qualified to compete at a show.
BR. Breeder.
BREED. Cats with similar physical characteristics and related ancestry.
BREED STANDARDS. Ideal standards for a particular breed as formulated by a cat association.
BRUSH. The plumelike tail of a longhaired cat.
CALLING. The vocalizing of a female cat in season.
CAT FANCY. A name given to the hobby of purebred cats.
CAT FANCIER. One who either owns, breeds, and/or shows purebred cats.
CATALOG. The official show record.
CFA. Cat Fanciers' Association.
CFF. Cat Fanciers' Federation, Inc.
CH. Champion.
COLOSTRUM. A dam's first milk.
CYSTITIS. An inflammation of the bladder.
DAM. The mother of a cat.
DECLAW. To surgically remove the claws.
ENTRY CLERK. The club official who receives, processes, and confirms all entries to a show.
ESTRUS. The sexually receptive period of a female cat during which she can become pregnant. Also "heat" or "in season."

EXHIBITOR. A person who shows a cat.

FELINE CALCIVIRUS (FVC). A viral illness affecting the respiratory system.

FELINE CHLAMYDIOSIS (FC). A bacteria-caused respiratory illness.

FELINE IMMUNODEFICIENCY VIRUS (FIV). An illness similar to human AIDS, attacking the body's immune system.

FELINE INFECTIOUS PERITONITIS (FIP). An almost-always fatal viral cat disease.

FELINE LEUKEMIA VIRUS (FeLV). An infectious disease that weakens the body, allowing the entry of other diseases, which are ultimately fatal.

FELINE PANLEUKOPENIA (FP). A viral disease also known as distemper and infectious enteritis.

FELINE UROLOGIC SYNDROME (FUS). Diseases of the urinary tract such as cystitis, blockage, or kidney stones.

FELINE VIRAL RHINOTRACHEITIS (FVR). A disease affecting the respiratory tract.

GATE. The paying visitors of a cat show.

GESTATION. The period of pregnancy in a cat.

GC. Grand Champion.

GP. Grand Premier.

JUDGE. A person licensed by a cat association to judge the entries in a show.

KITTEN. A feline under the age of eight months.

LITTER. Kittens born at the same time with the same parents.

LITTER REGISTRATION. A cat association's record of the birth of a litter, specifying the date of birth, the number of kittens, the sire and the dam, their colors and registration numbers.

LONGHAIR. One of the two groups into which cats are divided.

MASTITIS. Inflammation of the mammary gland.

METESTRUS. The period following estrus, during which the queen's sexual appetite wanes.

MGC. Master Grand Champion.

NEUTER. A male cat who has been altered.

OVULATE. The release of an egg from the ovary.

OVUM. The egg (plural: ova).

OW. Owner.

OXYTOCIN. A hormone used to stimulate uterine contractions.

PAPERS. A cat's registration and pedigree.

PARTURITION. The act of labor or birth.

PEDIGREE. The "family tree," listing the names, colors, titles, and registration numbers of a cat's predecessors for three, four, or five generations.

PH. Photographer.

POLYDACTYL. Having extra toes.

PROESTRUS. The period preceding estrus.

PROGESTERONE. A hormone that prepares the uterus for pregnancy.

PUREBRED. A member of a recognized breed whose lineage has remained pure or unmixed.

PREMIER. For show purposes, an altered cat of either sex.

PR. Premier.

QUEEN. A breeding female cat.

REGISTRATION. The recording of a cat's name and owner in a cat association; a certificate of same is issued to the owner.

Registration Number. A specific number assigned to a specific cat by the association.

REGISTRY. A cat association or federation.

RING. The place where a competition is judged by one judge.

SCABIES. A mite infestation of the skin.

SGC. Senior Grand Champion.

SHORTHAIR. One of two groups into which cats are divided.

SHOW FLYER. A paper containing information about an upcoming show.

SIRE. The father of a litter.

SPAY. A female who has had her reproductive organs surgically removed.

SPRAYING. A cat's habit of marking with urine his or her territory.

STUD. A breeding male cat.

STUD TAIL. Excessive oil production on the tail.

TAURINE. An amino acid vital to a cat's eyes and heart.

TESTOSTERONE. A male sex hormone produced in the testes.

TOXOPLASMOSIS. A disease spread by cats and other small animals, particularly dangerous to pregnant women.

TICA. The International Cat Association.

TYPE. The desirable physical appearance of a particular breed (bone structure, nose, eyes, tail length, etc.) as defined by each association.

VULVA. The entrance to the vagina.

WHOLE MALE. A male that has not been neutered.

ZOONITIC. Of a disease infectious from animal to human.

BIBLIOGRAPHY

Allaby, Michael. *Your Cat's First Year.* New York: Simon and Schuster, 1985.

Belfield, Wendell O., D.V.M. and Martin Zucker. *The Very Healthy Cat Book.* New York: McGraw-Hill, 1981.

Brearley, Joan McDonald. *All About Himalayan Cats.* Neptune City, N.J.: t.f.h. Publications, Inc., 1976.

Caras, Roger. *A Celebration of Cats.* New York: Simon and Schuster, 1986.

———. *Harper's Illustrated Handbook of Cats.* New York: Harper and Row, 1985.

Carr, William H. A. *The New Basic Book of The Cat.* New York: Scribner's Sons, 1978.

Cornell Feline Health Center Faculty and Staff. *The Cornell Book of Cats,* edited by Mordecai Siegal. New York: Villard Books, 1991.

Fogarty, Marna. *The Cat Fanciers' Association Annual Yearbook.* Manasquan, NJ: The Cat Fanciers' Association, Inc., 1976–1992.

Fox, Dr. Michael W. *The New Animal Doctor's Answer Book.* New York: Newmarket Press, 1984.

———. *Understanding Your Cat.* New York: Bantam Books, 1974.

Frazier, Anitra, with Norma Eckroate. *The Natural Cat.* New York: Kampmann and Co., 1981.

Kritsick, Stephen M., D.V.M. *Dr. Kritsick's Tender Loving Cat Care.* New York: Simon and Schuster, 1987.

Loxton, Howard. *The Noble Cat.* New York: Portland House, 1990.

Manolson, Frank, D.V.M. *My Cat's in Love.* New York: St. Martin's Press, 1970.

McGinnis, Terri, D.V.M. *The Well Cat Book.* San Francisco: The Bookworks. New York: Random House, Inc., 1975.

Necker, Claire. *The Natural History of Cats.* South Brunswick and New York: A. S. Barnes and Co., 1970.

Orchard, Marjorie M. *The Himalayan and Its Genetics.* Publisher Marjorie Orchard, 1979.

Pond, Grace. *The Complete Cat Encyclopedia.* New York: Crown Publishers, 1979.

Randolph, Elizabeth. *How to Be Your Cat's Best Friend.* New York: Fawcett Crest, 1981.

Siegel, Mordecai. *The Good Cat Book.* New York: Fireside Books, 1981.

———. *Simon and Schuster's Guide to Cats.* New York: Simon and Schuster, 1983.

Sproule, Anna and Michael. *The Complete Book of the Cat.* New York: Gallery Books, 1987.

Taylor, David. *You and Your Cat.* New York: Alfred A. Knopf, 1990.

Vine, Louis L., D.V.M. *Common Sense Book of Complete Cat Care.* New York: Wm. Morrow Co., 1978.

Whitney, Leon, F., D.V.M. *The Complete Book of Cat Care.* New York: Doubleday and Company, 1950.

Wright, Michael, and Walters, Sally, eds. *The Book of the Cat.* New York: Summit Books, 1980.

BREEDER CREDITS

American Bobtail
Lisa Black, Bebop Cattery, Morrison, IL
Alain Guillerme, New York City, NY

American Shorthair
Ingeborg Urcia, Katzenburg, Cheney, WA
Cherise Jolley, Provo, UT

Bengal
Terri Pattison, Windstorm Bengals, Warrington, PA

Birman
Julie Collin, Pleasantview Birmans, Mt. Pleasant, MI

Chinchilla
Denise Foster, Rancho Palos Verdes, CA

Cornish Rex
Diane Straka, DNA Cattery, Rochester, MN

Egyptian Mau
Tobe Goldman, Temek Cattery, Framingham, MA

Exotic Shorthair
The Bookbinders, Cakebread Exotics, Cincinnati, OH

Himalayan
Gena Windham, Hiwind Himalayans, Oceanside, CA
Elaine Gilbertson, Rajapur Himalayans, Vista, CA

Japanese Bobtail
Janet Bassetti, Bassetti's, Vineland, NJ
Cherise Jolley, Provo, UT

Maine Coon
Elizabeth Bannenberger, Dansway, Oceanside, CA

Norwegian Forest Cat
Louise Clair, Maineline Cattery, Corinth, TX

Persian
Cherie Lightner, GotTheLook Cattery, Bonita, CA

Russian Blue
Ingeborg Urcia, Katzenburg, Cheney, WA

Scottish Fold
Linda Rader, Shadyshack Cattery, Marshfield, MO

Siamese
Henri Pelletier, Gotier, Fort Lauderdale, FL

Siberian
Elizabeth Terrell, Starpoint, Baton Rouge, LA

Singapura
Douglas Pollock, Sayang Singapuras, Key West, FL

Snowshoe
Bonnie Butcher, Magnum Cattery, Denver, CO

Somali
Karen Stebner, Diamondust, Sandy, UT

Sphynx
Kathy Speed, Jokatta, Benton, MS

Tonkinese
Eileen Fusci, Fewsee Felines, Hollis, NH

Turkish Van
Ann Van Brunt, Lotsaluvan Turkish Vans, Grandview, MO

PHOTOGRAPHER CREDITS

Cornish Rex
Courtesy Vickie Jackson, New Orleans, LA

Egyptian Mau
Courtesy David Eckard, Westminster, MA

Himalayan Kittens/Author
Ron Burgis, Solana Beach, CA
Expressly Portraits

Japanese Bobtail
Courtesy Mark McCullough, Ballwin, MO

Maine Coon
Olin Mills

Norwegian Forest Cat
Courtesy Tetsu Yamazaki, Japan

Scottish Fold
Courtesy Mark McCullough, Ballwin, MO

Singapura
Courtesy Douglas Pollock, Key West, FL

Somali
Courtesy Carl J. Widmer, Los Gatos, CA

Sphynx
Courtesy Tetsu Yamazaki, Japan

Turkish Van
Courtesy Mark McCullough, Ballwin, MO

INDEX